KU-181-529

The Soviet Union in World Politics

'. . . an excellent short survey of Soviet foreign policy from World War II
to the collapse of the USSR.'

Robert V. Daniels, University of Vermont

The Soviet Union played a decisive role in defining the shape and pattern of world politics for nearly fifty years following the end of the
Second World War. *The Soviet Union in World Politics* provides an out-
line of Soviet foreign policy and international relations from 1945,
through the cold war to the break up of the USSR.

Geoffrey Roberts considers the global and internal impact of Soviet
policies and includes discussion of:

* the origins and development of the cold war
* the German question, the Korean War and the Sino-Soviet split
* the role of ideology
* how the cold war with the USSR ended
* problems of evidence and the new availability of archives

With a useful guide to further reading and a chronology of events, *The
Soviet Union in World Politics* debates key issues of Soviet global and
national politics and assesses the impact and legacy of this superpower
on the world stage.

Geoffrey Roberts is Lecturer in Modern History at University College
Cork, Ireland.

The Making of the Contemporary World
Edited by Eric Evans and Ruth Henig
University of Lancaster

The Making of the Contemporary World series provides challenging interpretations of contemporary issues and debates within strongly defined historical frameworks. The range of the series is global, with each volume drawing together material from a range of disciplines – including economics, politics and sociology. The books in this series present compact, indispensable introductions for students studying the modern world.

Titles include:

The Uniting of Europe
From Discord to Concord
Stanley Henig

International Economy since 1945
Sidney Pollard

United Nations in the Contemporary World
David Whittaker

Latin America
John Ward

Thatcher and Thatcherism
Eric J. Evans

Decolonization
Raymond F. Betts

China Under Communism
Alan Lawrance

Pacific Asia
Yumei Zhang

Conflicts in the Middle East since 1945
Beverley Milton-Edwards and Peter Hinchcliffe

The Irish Question
Patrick Maume

Right-Wing Extremism
Paul Hainsworth

The Green Movement
Dick Richardson

Forthcoming titles:

The Cold War
An Interdisciplinary History
David Painter

Multinationals
Peter Wardley

Nationalism and State
Malcolm Anderson

The Soviet Union in World Politics

Coexistence, Revolution and
Cold War, 1945–1991

Geoffrey Roberts

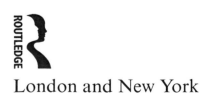

London and New York

BLACKBURN COLLEGE
LIBRARY

Acc. No. BB52531

Class No.UCL 909 : 825 ROB

Date 5 - 11 - 2012

First published 1999
by Routledge
2 Park Square, Milton Park, Abingdon, Oxon, OX14 4RN

Simultaneously published in the USA and Canada
by Routledge
270 Madison Ave, New York NY 10016

Transferred to Digital Printing 2008

© 1999 Geoffrey Roberts

Typeset in Times by
M Rules

All rights reserved. No part of this book may be reprinted or
reproduced or utilised in any form or by any electronic,
mechanical, or other means, now known or hereafter
invented, including photocopying and recording, or in any
information storage or retrieval system, without permission in
writing from the publishers.

British Library Cataloguing in Publication Data
A catalogue record for this book is available from the British Library

Library of Congress Cataloging in Publication Data
Roberts, Geoffrey K.
   The Soviet Union in World politics: coexistence,
   revolution, and cold war, 1945–1991/Geoffrey Roberts.
      p.   cm. — (Making of the contemporary world)
   Includes bibliographical references and index.
   1. Soviet Union—Foreign relations—1945–1991.
   2. World Politics—1945– 3. Cold War. I. Title. II. Series.
   DK267.R468 1999   98–28013
   909.82'5—dc21   CIP

ISBN 0–415–19246–3 (hbk)
ISBN 0–415–14435–3 (pbk)

To Celia

Contents

Maps

Acknowledgements

This is a work of synthesis rather than original research. So my first acknowledgement has to be to the generations of scholars who have explored in detail the complexities and intricacies of postwar Soviet foreign policy. I have tried to indicate my main sources of inspiration by references in the text and in the comments in the guide to further reading.

I would like to thank Caroline Kennedy-Pipe and Dennis Ogden for their detailed and illuminating comments on the draft of the book. The reports of Routledge's referees were also extremely helpful.

Others who played a part in the realisation of this project include the series editors, Eric Evans and Ruth Henig, who invited me to make a contribution to *The Making of the Contemporary World* series, and Routledge's History Editor, Heather McCallum, who gently nudged the book to completion.

I have benefited greatly from supervising the research of a number of postgraduates at University College Cork (UCC), in particular those postgraduates who worked on aspects of postwar Soviet foreign policy: Caroline Buckley, David Lyons, Brian McGee and Brendan Quinn. Of value, too, was the experience of teaching an undergraduate option course on 'The Soviet Union in World Politics'. The Department of History at UCC has continued to provide a very congenial atmosphere in which to work.

As always with my published work, the whole text was carefully edited and commented upon by Celia Weston. For this reason, and many others, I dedicate the book to her.

Note on references

In the text I have used the Harvard reference system in which citations take the form of author's surname followed by year of publication of the book or article. The idea is that the reader can then refer to the bibliography for full publication details. As the bibliography is divided into four sections, I have indicated which references are to articles or memoirs. Otherwise, all citations refer to publications in the books section.

Chronology of highlights in Soviet foreign policy, 1945–91

1945

May: Red Army occupies Berlin
August: Hiroshima and Nagasaki A-bombed by the United States

1946

March: Churchill's 'iron curtain' speech in Fulton, Missouri
July–October: Paris peace conference

1947

March: Truman Doctrine speech
September: Zhdanov two-camps speech at the founding conference of
    the Cominform

1948

June: Soviet blockade of Berlin (ends May 1949)
June: Stalin–Tito split: Yugoslav Communist Party expelled from the
Cominform

1949

January: Establishment of the Council for Mutual Economic Assistance
    (CMEA)
April: Signature of North Atlantic Treaty Organisation (NATO) treaty
May: Establishment of the Federal Republic of Germany
August: Soviet A-bomb test
October: Proclamation of the People's Republic of China
October: Establishment of the German Democratic Republic

1950

February: Signature of Sino-Soviet treaty of alliance
June: Outbreak of the Korean War

1953

March: Death of Stalin
June: Popular uprising in East Germany
August: Announcement of Soviet H-Bomb test

1955

May: Signature of the Warsaw Pact
July: Geneva summit of Britain, France, the Soviet Union and the US

1956

February: Twentieth congress of the Communist Party of the Soviet Union (CPSU)
October–November: Soviet military intervention in Hungary

1958

November: Khrushchev ultimatum on Berlin

1960

April: Sino-Soviet split develops

1961

August: Building of the Berlin Wall

1962

October: Cuban missile crisis

1964

October: Khrushchev deposed as Soviet leader

1968

August: Invasion of Czechoslovakia

1969

March: Military clashes along the Sino-Soviet border

1970

March: Nuclear Non-Proliferation Treaty comes into force

1972

May: Signature of first Strategic Arms Limitation Talks (SALT) treaty

1973

January: Paris agreement on ending the war in Vietnam

1975

August: Conference on Security and Co-operation in Europe (CSCE)
  agreement signed in Helsinki

1979

December: Soviet military intervention in Afghanistan

1980

August: Solidarity crisis in Poland

1981

December: Martial law declared in Poland

1985

March: Gorbachev elected General Secretary of the CPSU

1987

December: Signature of Intermediate Nuclear Forces (INF) treaty

1988

February: Announcement of Soviet withdrawal from Afghanistan

1989

November: Fall of the Berlin Wall

1990

October: Reunification of Germany

1991

June/July: Disbandment of the CMEA and the Warsaw Pact
August: Attempted coup by Soviet hardliners
December: Resignation of Gorbachev and dissolution of the USSR

Map 1 Divided Europe in 1949 (derived from P. Hastings, *The Cold War: 1945–69*, London, Ernest Benn, 1969)

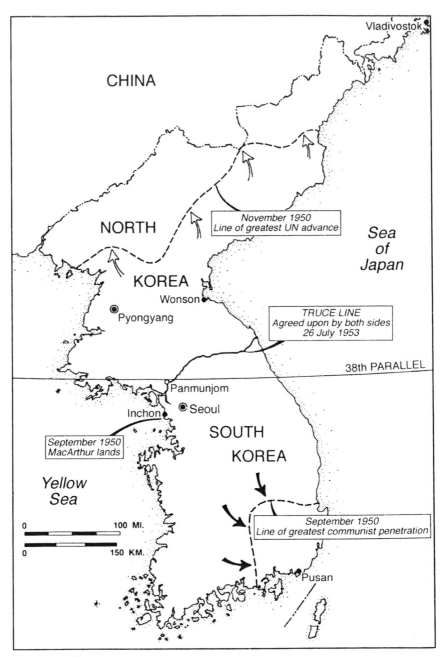

Map 2 Military phases of the Korean War, 1950–3 (derived from R.H. Ferrell (ed.) *America in a Divided World, 1945–1972*, New York, HarperCollins Publishers, Inc., © 1975 Robert H. Ferrell)

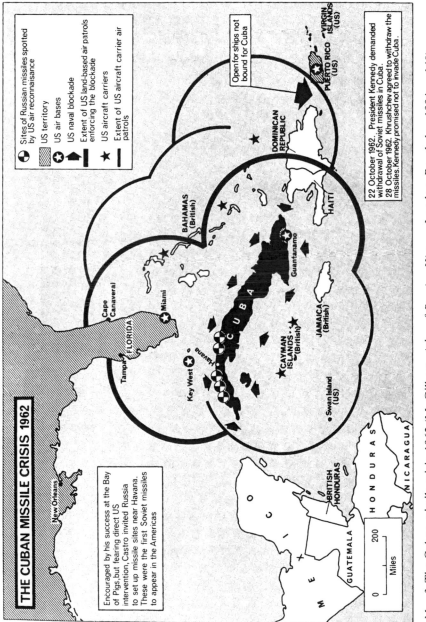

THE CUBAN MISSILE CRISIS 1962

Sites of Russian missiles spotted
by US air reconnaissance

US territory

US air bases

US naval blockade

Extent of US land-based air patrols
enforcing the blockade

US aircraft carriers

Extent of US aircraft carrier air
patrols

Open for ships not
bound for Cuba

22 October 1962. President Kennedy demanded
withdrawal of Soviet missiles in Cuba.
28 October 1962. Khrushchev agreed to withdraw the
missiles. Kennedy promised not to invade Cuba.

Encouraged by his success at the Bay
of Pigs, but fearing direct US
intervention, Castro invited Russia
to set up missile sites near Havana.
These were the first Soviet missiles
to appear in the Americas

New Orleans

FLORIDA
Cape
Canaveral
Tampa
Miami
Key West
HAVANA
C U B A
Guantanamo
CAYMAN
ISLANDS
(British)
JAMAICA
(British)
Swan Island
(US)
BAHAMAS
(British)
HAITI
DOMINICAN
REPUBLIC
PUERTO RICO
(US)
VIRGIN
ISLANDS
(US)

GUATEMALA
M E
BRITISH
HONDURAS
H O N D U R A S
NICARAGUA

0   200
Miles

Map 3 The Cuban missile crisis, 1962 (M. Gilbert, *Atlas of Russian History*, London, Routledge, 1994, p. 140)

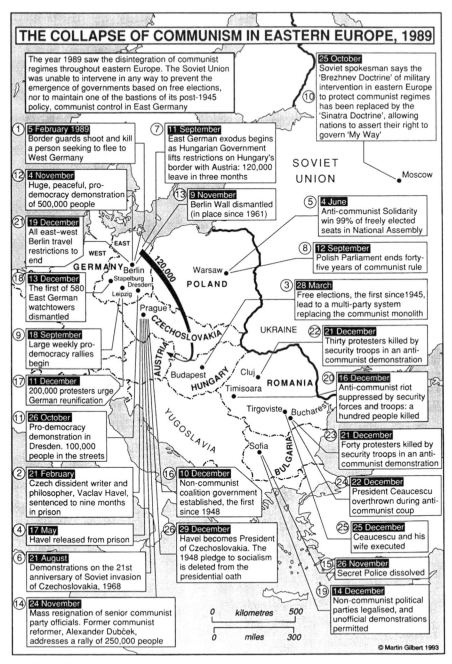

THE COLLAPSE OF COMMUNISM IN EASTERN EUROPE, 1989

The year 1989 saw the disintegration of communist regimes throughout eastern Europe. The Soviet Union was unable to intervene in any way to prevent the emergence of governments based on free elections, nor to maintain one of the bastions of its post-1945 policy, communist control in East Germany

(10) 25 October
Soviet spokesman says the 'Brezhnev Doctrine' of military intervention in eastern Europe to protect communist regimes has been replaced by the 'Sinatra Doctrine', allowing nations to assert their right to govern 'My Way'

(1) 5 February 1989
Border guards shoot and kill a person seeking to flee to West Germany

(7) 11 September
East German exodus begins as Hungarian Government lifts restrictions on Hungary's border with Austria: 120,000 leave in three months

SOVIET
UNION

Moscow

(12) 4 November
Huge, peaceful, pro-democracy demonstration of 500,000 people

(13) 9 November
Berlin Wall dismantled (in place since 1961)

(5) 4 June
Anti-communist Solidarity win 99% of freely elected seats in National Assembly

(21) 19 December
All east–west Berlin travel restrictions to end

(8) 12 September
Polish Parliament ends forty-five years of communist rule

WEST
EAST
GERMANY Berlin
Stapelburg
Dresden
Leipzig
Warsaw •
POLAND
Prague
CZECHOSLOVAKIA
AUSTRIA
120,000

(18) 13 December
The first of 580 East German watchtowers dismantled

UKRAINE

(3) 28 March
Free elections, the first since 1945, lead to a multi-party system replacing the communist monolith

(9) 18 September
Large weekly pro-democracy rallies begin

(22) 21 December
Thirty protesters killed by security troops in an anti-communist demonstration

(17) 11 December
200,000 protesters urge German reunification

Budapest
HUNGARY
Cluj •
Timisoara
ROMANIA
Tirgoviste • Bucharest

(20) 16 December
Anti-communist riot suppressed by security forces and troops: a hundred people killed

(11) 26 October
Pro-democracy demonstration in Dresden. 100,000 people in the streets

YUGOSLAVIA

(23) 21 December
Forty protesters killed by security troops in an anti-communist demonstration

(2) 21 February
Czech dissident writer and philosopher, Vaclav Havel, sentenced to nine months in prison

(16) 10 December
Non-communist coalition government established, the first since 1948

Sofia
BULGARIA

(24) 22 December
President Ceaucescu overthrown during anti-communist coup

(4) 17 May
Havel released from prison

(26) 29 December
Havel becomes President of Czechoslovakia. The 1948 pledge to socialism is deleted from the presidential oath

(25) 25 December
Ceaucescu and his wife executed

(6) 21 August
Demonstrations on the 21st anniversary of Soviet invasion of Czechoslovakia, 1968

(15) 26 November
Secret Police dissolved

(19) 14 December
Non-communist political parties legalised, and unofficial demonstrations permitted

(14) 24 November
Mass resignation of senior communist party officials. Former communist reformer, Alexander Dubček, addresses a rally of 250,000 people

0	kilometres	500
0	miles	300

© Martin Gilbert 1993

Map 4 The collapse of communism in eastern Europe, 1989 (M. Gilbert, *Atlas of Russian History*, London, Routledge, 1994, p. 152)

1 Perspectives on postwar Soviet foreign policy

INTRODUCTION

For nearly 50 years after the Second World War the Soviet Union played a decisive role in defining the shape and pattern of world politics. Before the Second World War the Soviet state was only an intermittently important actor in European politics, often ignored or marginalised by the other great powers. After the war, however, the Soviet Union came to head a powerful military-political bloc of states in eastern Europe. In the 1960s and 1970s the Soviet Union emerged as a global, nuclear superpower – involved in all the major developments, issues and crises of world politics. At the same time the Soviet Union remained a communist state, officially committed to the establishment of a global socialist system. Indeed, at times during the postwar period – as Soviet and communist influence spread across the world – it seemed that Moscow's trumpeting of the historical inevitability of socialism was more than mere hyperbole. In the late 1980s, however, it was not capitalism but communism that collapsed, first in eastern Europe and then in the Soviet Union itself.

The dramatic fall of communism and then the break up, in 1991, of the Union of Soviet Socialist Republics (USSR) – the multinational state ruled by the communists for over 70 years – was a surprising end to a story that begins (for the purposes of this text) with the Soviet victory over Nazi Germany in 1945. The Red Army's repulse of the German invasion of Russia and its victorious march to Berlin was the mightiest feat of arms the world had ever known. The communist system survived the supreme test of war and, by the end of hostilities, the Red Army occupied half of Europe. Stalin, the Soviet dictator, was a figure of admiration and adulation at home and abroad. Across the continent there was a massive upsurge of popular support for communism and left-wing politics. In these circumstances no one doubted the importance and centrality of the USSR to the future of domestic and foreign politics in Europe.

But the USSR was not the only victor of the Second World War, and not the only arbiter of the peace. In 1945 it was expected that the wartime coalition of Britain, the Soviet Union and the United States would continue in peacetime – that the Grand Alliance which had won the war would jointly shape and safeguard a new, peaceful, postwar world order. That was the prospect proclaimed by the leaders of the Grand Alliance at the Yalta and Potsdam conferences and the vision acclaimed by the citizenry of the victorious allied nations. But the peacetime Grand Alliance proved to be short-lived. By 1947–8 what was called a 'cold war' broke out between the Soviet Union and its erstwhile coalition partners. From that point on, the postwar history of Soviet foreign policy was intimately bound up with the USSR's involvement in the cold war.

SOVIET FOREIGN POLICY AND THE COLD WAR

The 'cold war' is a term that refers to the state of tension, hostility, competition and conflict which characterised Soviet–western, and more particularly, Soviet–American, relations for much of the postwar period. The most overt face of the cold war was the east–west division of Germany, a Europe divided by the so-called 'iron curtain' into competing liberal-democratic and communist camps, and the emergence of two antagonistic military-political alliances, NATO and the Warsaw Pact. Then there were the great international crises of the cold war era – Berlin, Korea, Cuba, Vietnam – which at times seemed to threaten the outbreak of a new world war. Adding to the drama of these moments of cold war confrontation was the perception of a deeper economic, political and ideological competition between the Soviet and western blocs – a competition not just of power blocs but between capitalism and socialism, between different socio-economic and cultural systems and traditions.

To those who fought the cold war – the much-maligned 'cold warriors' – there was far more at stake than geopolitical position or economic interests. The 'other side' was viewed as threatening not just vital interests, but one's core values and identity as well. In the Soviet case the stakes were seen as high indeed: the survival of the socialist system, the maintenance of working-class power and communist party leadership, humanity's future in a collectivist, communist utopia.

But, sharp and intense as the conflict was, both sides had an interest in constraining the cold war, in limiting and controlling the rivalry and competition, in achieving a degree of stability, order and predictability in world politics. Not the least compelling reason for containing the conflict was the existence of nuclear weapons – which threatened mutual annihilation in the event of the outbreak of a 'hot war' between the great powers. There were also various economic, political and ideological incentives to relax the tension, to foster what became known in the 1960s as 'détente'. Peace was, among other things, good for trade, good propaganda value and good for domestic and international political prestige.

The history of the cold war is a story, as John Lewis Gaddis has put it (Gaddis, 1987), of a 'long peace', as well as a protracted and dangerous conflict, of strivings for co-operation as well as competitive advantage. Indeed, conceptualising postwar international relations purely in terms of the cold war is a very western perspective. Viewed from Moscow, the story of postwar Soviet–western relations should, perhaps, be recast as a story of the struggle for peaceful coexistence and détente interrupted by the periodic outbreaks of cold war.

It is conventional to date the cold war as lasting from the mid-1940s to the late 1980s. But, as we shall see, for many of those years something approximating a détente (or attempts at a détente) was characteristic of east–west relations. Much of the 1950s, most of the 1960s, the first half of the 1970s and the second half of the 1980s were periods of reducing international tension, indeed of political and ideological relaxation in the capitalist–communist struggle.

From the Soviet leadership's point of view – from Stalin to Gorbachev – the periodic outbursts of cold war were something thrust upon them by an aggressive and threatening western alliance. Their preferred option was the coexistence of capitalism and socialism, mutually beneficial co-operation between the two systems, and peaceful competition to determine which side was economically, socially and culturally superior. Of course, Moscow believed in and desired the achievement of socialism on a world-wide scale and saw the building of the communist system in the USSR as part of an inexorable historical transition from capitalism to socialism. The Soviet leadership believed, too, that peaceful coexistence and détente provided a favourable context for the revolutionary struggle for socialism in the capitalist and imperialist world – a struggle which the Soviet Union would aid ideologically, politically and materially. But, so the Soviets believed, the future march of history did not mean that you could not do business with the capitalists in the present, nor did it preclude inter-state and inter-system co-operation on matters of common interest.

PEACEFUL COEXISTENCE AND REVOLUTION

As its subtitle and contents indicate, this book is organised around the dual theme of the Soviet pursuit of peaceful coexistence and the linked aspiration to the revolutionary spread of socialism on a world-wide scale. This doctrine-cum-policy of 'peaceful coexistence' dated back to the early 1920s when the Bolshevik revolutionaries who had seized power in the Tsarist Russian Empire in 1917 began to seek a *modus vivendi* with the capitalist world. The capitalist states which the Bolsheviks sought to develop relations with were the same countries that had aided their 'counter-revolutionary' enemies in the Russian civil war of 1918–21. At first, therefore, the pursuit of peaceful coexistence was conceived as a short-term tactic designed to inhibit further capitalist attacks on the USSR, pending the spread of revolution to other countries. But, as the prospect of world revolution receded even further, as the peace with the capitalist states lasted longer than expected, and as the building of socialism in the USSR came to assume ever-greater priority, a temporary tactic was transformed into a permanent strategy. Socialism in the USSR would be safeguarded not by the revolutionary overthrow of capitalism on a world-wide scale but by peaceful coexistence with the capitalist states.

After the Second World War the doctrine of peaceful coexistence underwent many modifications. Of prime importance in the early postwar years was the fact that the socialist camp now consisted not of an isolated and vulnerable USSR, but a bloc of communist-controlled countries headed by an emerging global superpower. Peaceful coexistence was, therefore, recast in more assertive and aggressive terms as a relationship imposed on capitalism and imperialism by the superior strength of socialist forces. In the 1950s, more and more emphasis came to be placed on peaceful coexistence as a means of avoiding a catastrophic nuclear war that would make redundant the political and economic competition between the socialist and capitalist systems. In the 1960s and 1970s – in the heyday of détente – peaceful coexistence came to mean positive co-operation, collaboration and interchange with the west. But that did not mean the abandonment of the USSR's global socialist aspirations; détente was seen as part of the process of consolidating the position of the socialist camp and as the harbinger of further shifts to the left in world politics. The revolutionary-political dimension of peaceful coexistence was abandoned only in the very last years of the Soviet regime when the communist reformer Mikhail Gorbachev radically redefined the USSR as a status quo power committed more to the spread of humanism than socialism.

This focusing on peaceful coexistence as an ideology of coexistence and revolution is only one way of conceptualising postwar Soviet foreign policy. It should certainly not be seen as providing a neat explanation for everything Moscow did in the international arena. Peaceful coexistence was a doctrinal and strategic context for action – a referential framework for the main orientations of Soviet foreign policy, not a dictator of specific decisions. To explain the particular actions and patterns of Soviet foreign policy it is necessary to take other factors into account. In order to tease out some of these other explanatory factors it will be useful to consider some alternative perspectives on the main thrust and pattern of Soviet foreign policy in the postwar period. These we will call the perspectives of 'security', 'power', 'ideology' and 'politics'.

SECURITY, POWER, IDEOLOGY AND POLITICS

The security perspective is the view that the driving force of Soviet foreign policy was the search for national security in what was perceived to be a hostile and threatening world. The cold war, it should be noted, was always an unequal struggle, which the Soviet Union waged from a position of relative economic and military weakness. Within this perspective the emphasis is on the defensive and reactive character of Moscow's foreign decision-making, on the limits of Soviet international ambitions, and the centrality of security considerations to calculations of foreign policy.

This security perspective has much to commend it: it captures the essential insecurity of the Soviet orientation to the outside world; focuses attention on the very real national security issues and dilemmas confronting Moscow; and provides an analytical key to explain most, if not all, the major acts of postwar Soviet foreign policy. The limitation of this perspective is that it underestimates the extent to which the USSR was a revolutionary state committed to a radical transformation of the international status quo. Such a commitment meant that in practice the USSR pursued political aims which went far beyond what was required for the sake of security. It meant continued adherence to a Marxist-Leninist view of international relations and world politics. It meant proclaiming and speaking the language of revolutionary politics. All this lent Soviet foreign policy a very particular and peculiar character – one which eludes analysis solely in terms of traditional diplomacy and statecraft in pursuit of national security.

Calculations, relations and necessities of power dominate the second of the two perspectives. The power perspective is the view that, in the postwar period, the Soviet Union was locked in a power struggle with the United States. That power struggle was a consequence of the Second World War which saw the destruction of the traditional European state-system, the decline and fall of the European great powers and the creation of a geopolitical power vacuum in the very heart of Europe which was filled by the emergent competing interests of the American and Soviet superpowers. In this view the cold war conflict was characterised by the pursuit of power as a means of achieving security in the face of the threat of expansionary encroachments by the other side.

Viewing the cold war as a power contest has its attractions. Power calculations and manoeuvres were certainly an important dimension of postwar Soviet foreign policy. Like their counterparts in the west, the Soviets fought the cold war with the aim of gaining a competitive edge that was, more often than not, defined in power terms. It is also true that the available resources of power – military, political, economic – could be either a crucial constraint on *or* an enabler of action. The power perspective can also help to explain how it was that the cold war became a global rivalry and competition. The cold war game of seeking power and influence knew no geographical bounds.

But recognising the power factor in Soviet foreign policy, in the cold war and in world politics is not the same as endorsing the power perspective. That would require the endorsement of one or other version of 'realism' – the view that international relations is fundamentally about power politics, that the actions of states are best understood in terms of systems and relations of power. However, Soviet foreign policy is better conceived as being part of a system of action and interaction rather than a structure of power. Soviet policy-makers acted within a context which was not entirely of their making and over which they had only limited control. But the most important part of that context consisted of other human actors, their actions and the states and organisations they represented. The cold war was a human conflict that was initiated, sustained and brought to an end by human beings acting on the basis of changed perceptions and attitudes. Of course, sometimes Soviet actions conformed (or appeared to conform) to realist power-politics models of state behaviour, but often they did not. It is impossible, for example, to explain Gorbachev's foreign policy actions – his voluntary relinquishment of vital Soviet interests and positions – within a realist framework of analysis. Gorbachev's giving up of power can be explained away by realist analysis, but not truly accounted for by it. To explain Gorbachev's foreign policy it is necessary to refer to the revolution in Soviet ideology that occurred after he became leader.

Both the security and the power perspectives would tend to downplay the role of ideology in Soviet foreign policy. 'Ideology' in this context refers to the Soviet regime's official doctrine of Marxism-Leninism and associated views and analyses of international relations and foreign policy. Ideology's role was to define certain international goals for the Soviet state and to act as the conceptual framework through which to filter perceptions and experience.

One example of an ideology perspective on Soviet foreign policy is this book, whose basic argument is that ideologically informed conceptions of peaceful coexistence provided a strategic context of action for Soviet decision-makers. But there are other perspectives – which offer competing accounts of what the content of Soviet ideology was and how it related to policy practice. For example, a view popular in the west during the cold war era was that the USSR was a state driven by a messianic ideology which directed a programme of territorial and political expansionism in order to achieve a communist world in the Soviet Union's own image. Variations of that view included the argument that Soviet communist ideology was reinforced by a pre-existing tradition of foreign expansionism – notably, Tsarist Russia's drive for security by the occupation of space. Yet others emphasised the importance of the Marxist-Leninist conceptual apparatus which viewed world politics in terms of capitalism, imperialism and the class struggle.

What unites these different accounts of the role of ideology is the view that the self-proclaimed ideological bases of Soviet foreign policy should be taken seriously. The USSR was an ideological state. It had an ideologically driven programme for the transformation of world politics; an ideological view of international relations; and an ideological self-image of Soviet foreign policy. The great strength of an ideology perspective is that it is able to focus on what is most obvious about Soviet foreign policy: its ideological character. The main problem with this perspective is that while it might offer a series of plausible explanations and interpretations of Soviet foreign policy, the connections posited between abstract ideas and concrete foreign policy actions are often difficult to establish. While there is sometimes clear evidence of ideological motive and reasoning, it is often impossible to disentangle the ideological factor from calculations of power and security in the making of Soviet foreign policy.

Another problem for this perspective is that while ideology may be the prompter and shaper of action it also, in the Soviet case, performed a complex of other functions: political propaganda, policy legitimation, popular mobilisation domestically and internationally. To what extent, then, was ideology an instrument rather than a shaper of Soviet foreign and domestic policy? Nor is specifying the content of the ideology without its difficulties because Soviet ideology was not static but ever-changing, subject to different interpretations by its adherents, and not always internally consistent and coherent. Finally, ideology is a very individual and personal thing. The character and depth of ideological beliefs and commitments and how these express themselves in practice varies from person to person. The question always has to be posed: whose ideology, whose action, whose purpose?

The analysis of ideology is further complicated by considerations emanating from the politics perspective on Soviet foreign policy. This is the view that emphasises the role of internal factional struggles in determining foreign policy. In some cases these struggles are between individuals and groups with different standpoints on foreign policy – clashes between those with genuine differences of perception, calculation and opinion. In other cases, however, it is possible to identify different interests and interest groups in the making of Soviet foreign policy. Crudely put, the basic idea is that people say and do things in order to protect and enhance their power, position and privileges. Within this perspective, Soviet foreign policy is analysed as the outcome of a contest between individuals and groups pursuing their own interest-driven agendas. This kind of approach is often linked to perceptions of internal factional struggles over Soviet foreign policy which derive from different institutions and their conflicting interests: militaristic hawks in the armed forces, diplomatic doves in the foreign ministry; ideological hardliners in the communist party apparatus, pragmatists in government organisations; managers and technocrats in the defence industries versus those in consumer industries; and so on. A more general example of the politics perspective is the view that the cold war was a conflict whose perpetuation suited the interests of various Soviet elites and institutions: the communist leadership who needed an excuse for the maintenance of their authoritarian rule; the military-industrial complex, which benefited from high levels of defence spending; the security and intelligence services with their need for an external enemy to combat; party ideologues with an interest in the continuation of a state of tension conducive to the maintenance of political orthodoxy.

Clearly, people (even communists!) often do act out of self-interest and use ideology, national interest, or whatever, to justify their aims and position. Equally, it is certainly possible to identify various groups and institutions in the USSR and to attribute to them different and conflicting interests in relation to foreign policy (although the map of such interests is highly complex and contradictory). One can also point to various debates about foreign policy in the USSR in which much special pleading is evident from individuals based in different parts of the Soviet foreign policy and national security bureaucracy. But the question always to be asked about bureaucratic politics is: does it matter? How important was personal and bureaucratic politics when it came to the big issues and decisive actions of Soviet foreign policy? The answer seems to be that interest-based factional politics rarely played a decisive role in the determination of policy. This was because there existed views, loyalties, commitments, principles and traditions which cut across and overrode such interests. Ideology and national security supplemented by power calculations were the mainsprings of Soviet foreign policy; interests and interest group politics were of only secondary importance, particularly when it came to radical shifts in policy.

EVIDENCE AND ARCHIVES

Debates about the respective roles of ideology, security, power and politics in Soviet foreign policy are nothing new; they have been going on for decades. Central to most of those debates have been issues of Soviet motivations and intentions. Standing in the way of their resolution has been the absence of evidence from the Soviet archives on what had been said, reported, discussed and decided behind the closed doors of the Kremlin and the foreign ministry. Since the end of the communist regime, however, a large number of confidential documents on Soviet foreign policy during the cold war years from party and state archives have been published. The archives themselves have been opened to scholars (although some important collections on top-level decision-making remain inaccessible to all but a privileged few researchers). Many memoirs of Soviet diplomats and politicians have been published in recent years. We are also fortunate to have at our disposal a number of pathbreaking books and articles on postwar Soviet foreign policy which make effective and judicious use of the newly available archive evidence.

What does this new material and new writing add to our knowledge and understanding of postwar Soviet foreign policy? The answer must be a matter of detailed exposition, discussion and argument. In a schematic and summary fashion this is one of the things this book attempts to do. But, without wishing to pre-empt the commentary in later chapters, it is possible at this stage to offer a few preliminary generalisations about what the archives have revealed.

First, however comfortable and convenient it might have been for some people in the past, the western cold war caricature of the Soviet

Union as an aggressive and expansionist power aiming at world domination can be definitely discarded. The archives reveal no such plans, intentions or ambitions. What in the west was interpreted as threatening Soviet behaviour was from Moscow's point of view defensive or reactive action or tactics designed to force a compromise or to encourage negotiations on contentious issues. (This is not to deny Moscow's global, ideological aspirations).

Second, there was no secret or hidden foreign policy agenda. Private discussions about foreign policy were commensurate with those which took place in the public domain, i.e. what was said in speeches, at party congresses, in articles in the press and specialist journals, and so on. Of course, Soviet diplomats and politicians (like their counterparts in the west) did not reveal all their thinking and calculations to the world. For tactical, political, diplomatic or security reasons there were some things that could not be said publicly. But, by and large, the public statement of Soviet foreign policy was, it seems, an accurate reflection of the actual reasoning and decisions of policy-makers.

Third, ideology mattered. The ideological commitments of Soviet leaders were genuine, ideological considerations figured prominently in internal discussions about foreign policy, and the language of policy and decision was ideological. This last is perhaps the most important revelation of all. Ideology was talked in private as well as in public. The language of ideology was the means of internal communication among the Soviet elite as well as its method of public discourse. This is another reason for taking ideology seriously as a determinant of Soviet foreign policy.

Fourth, within the Soviet bloc Moscow was not the only important political actor. Time and again the archives reveal the role played by other communist leaders in prompting, influencing, even forcing Soviet foreign policy decisions and action. Examples of such an input by local communist leaders include the outbreak of the Korean War, the building of the Berlin Wall and the Soviet invasions of Hungary in 1956, Czechoslovakia in 1968 and Afghanistan in 1980.

Fifth, stamped upon the character and conduct of Soviet foreign policy were the individual personalities and preferences of successive Soviet leaders. Foreign policy was the prerogative of the top leadership, particularly the General Secretary of the communist party. Postwar Soviet foreign policy falls into four main phases, each with its own persona, each of which correspond to the rule of the four main postwar Soviet leaders: Stalin, Khrushchev, Brezhnev and Gorbachev. The archives confirm the central and defining role of these leaders in foreign policy.

To state that the leader of the Soviet communist party was the most important foreign policy decision-maker is not exactly a surprising conclusion. Nor are the other points about revelations from the archives particularly startling. As Vojtech Mastny said (Mastny, 1996 p. 9), the greatest surprise to have come out of the Soviet archives is that there is no surprise, at least not so far.

This does not mean, however, that there is nothing new to say about the history of Soviet foreign policy. The new evidence has generated many new insights and some novel interpretations of Soviet policy in the postwar period. Equally important has been the use to which the new evidence can be put in helping us to resolve some of the long-standing disputes about the nature of Soviet foreign policy.

But perhaps the most important gain from the new evidence is that it has significantly enhanced our ability to see and understand the story of postwar Soviet foreign policy from Moscow's point of view. The world as it appeared to successive Soviet leaders may not be the same world that we see, but it is the world that they acted in. The reconstruction of that world – the world of the Kremlin and Soviet foreign policy – is the main task of this book.

NOTE: SOVIET FOREIGN POLICY DECISION-MAKING

The structure of Soviet foreign policy decision-making may be schematised as shown in the diagram.

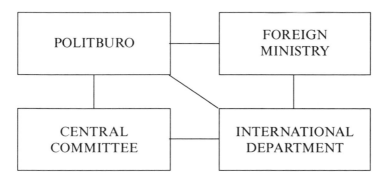

All the major decisions of postwar Soviet foreign policy were taken by the Politburo (or by Soviet leaders acting on its behalf). Implementation of decisions was mainly the responsibility of the Ministry of Foreign Affairs, which also had an important input into Politburo decision-making. The Politburo was the group of a dozen or so top leaders elected by the communist party central committee to control and direct the day-to-day affairs of the party and of the government. (Between 1952 and 1966 the Politburo was called the Presidium.) The central committee (several hundred members, elected by delegates to CPSU congresses) also had its own apparatus devoted to international affairs. The most important element of this apparatus was the International Department, which was responsible for the party's relations and links with foreign communist parties and with other 'progressive' organisations such as third world national liberation movements. Between 1957 and 1988 there was also a Socialist Countries Department, which was concerned with Soviet relations with the ruling parties of eastern Europe and other socialist states. These party organisations also contributed to the wider policy deliberations and decisions of the Politburo and the Foreign Ministry. Other agencies contributing to the policy process (sometimes crucially) included the Ministry of Defence, the armed forces, intelligence and security services (including the KGB), and specialist research institutes devoted to the study of foreign policy and international relations.

2 Coexistence, revolution and the cold war, 1945–56

> The Soviet Union has no intention of
> organising a Bolshevik revolution in
> Europe.
> (Stalin to Churchill, October 1944)

> This war is not as in the past; whoever
> occupies a territory also imposes on it
> his own social system. Everyone imposes
> his own system as far as his army can reach.
> It cannot be otherwise.
> (Stalin to Tito, April 1945)

OVERVIEW

Soviet foreign policy during the first postwar decade went through three main phases: a Grand Alliance phase (1945–7); a phase of cold war confrontation and polarisation (1947–50); and a phase of de-escalation and stabilisation of the cold war conflict (1950–6).

In the first two years after the war co-operation and negotiation between the Soviet Union, Great Britain and the United States continued. It was a period of intensive diplomatic contacts between Moscow, London and Washington. There were regular conferences between the foreign ministers of the 'Big Three'. Soviet and western diplomats worked constructively together in the newly created United Nations organisation. At the Paris peace conference in 1946, peace treaties with the former enemy states of Bulgaria, Finland, Hungary, Italy and Romania were successfully negotiated. This was also a time of allied co-operation at the Nuremberg trials of Nazi war criminals and of continuing hopes that it would be possible to devise and implement a common programme for the denazification, demilitarisation and democratisation of occupied Germany.

Of course, there were many tensions and contradictions, even crises, in relations between the USSR and its western coalition partners during this early postwar period; it is tempting to over-dramatise such conflicts and to read back into them the origins of the cold war. But at the time the diplomatic and political agenda of Soviet–western relations was still primarily a collaborative one, based on the assumption that the conflicts of interest and perspective were those of allies and that, with good will, the unity of the Grand Alliance would be maintained. Even Churchill in his notorious 'iron curtain' speech in Fulton, Missouri, in March 1946 did not challenge that assumption. The former Prime Minister denounced Russian and communist tyranny in eastern Europe and complained about the exclusion of western political influence from the region (that was the point about the 'iron curtain'). But Churchill also talked about the possible prolongation of the 1942 Anglo-Soviet treaty of alliance into a 50-year pact and of the need to reach a 'good understanding' with the USSR.

For their part, the Soviets constantly and consistently affirmed their commitment to making common cause with the British and Americans in a peacetime Grand Alliance. As late as May 1947 – on the very eve of the outbreak of the cold war – Stalin gave an interview to the US Republican Senator Harold Stassen in which he said: 'Not only can [the Soviet Union and the United States] coexist . . . they can also co-operate; if they did so during the war, why not now? Lenin said that the co-operation of the two systems was possible, and Lenin is our teacher' (Werth, 1971 p. 250).

The phase of cold war confrontation and polarisation dates from the middle of 1947. This was the period of the anti-communist Truman Doctrine speech, of the breakdown of east–west negotiations over the proposed Marshall Plan for US economic aid to Europe, and of the creation by Moscow of a new centre to direct and promote international communism – the Communist Information Bureau, or Cominform. These developments signalled the breakdown of the Grand Alliance relationship and the onset of the cold war. After the Cominform conference of European communist parties in September 1947 an anti-American campaign was launched by communists in western Europe. In eastern Europe the Soviet and communist grip on the region was extended radically. All opposition to communist rule was crushed, followed by the launch of programmes for the rapid introduction of Soviet-style socialism. Allied negotiations over the future of Germany broke down, leading to the establishment of separate East and West

German states and their respective integration into Soviet and western military-political blocs. In 1948–9 the Soviets blockaded the land routes into West Berlin, forcing an Anglo-American airlift to supply their sector of the jointly occupied German capital. This was the first of the great cold war crises. It was followed in June 1950 by – with Soviet blessing – communist North Korea's invasion of South Korea. The United States intervened in support of South Korea; in October 1950 'volunteers' from Communist China joined in the fight on the North Korean side. Although not formally involved in the war, the USSR was the main supplier of the communist forces in Korea, Soviet advisers played a key role in directing the North Korean war effort and Soviet pilots contributed significantly to the battle for air supremacy with the Americans.

Shortly before the outbreak of the war in Korea, Moscow and its communist movement allies had launched a big 'peace campaign'. It was an attempt to mobilise public opinion in the west against the 'Bomb' and the threat of a new world war. This peace campaign was, in fact, more indicative of the main direction of Soviet foreign policy than was the Korean adventure. The early 1950s was a period of Soviet attempts to put a brake on the cold war polarisation of Europe into opposing camps. Moscow made many proposals for the neutralisation and demilitarisation of central Europe, including proposals for a united but disarmed and neutral Germany. Plans for collective security arrangements covering the whole of Europe were also put forward, including a proposal, in 1954, that the USSR should become a member of NATO! Whether these were genuine efforts at détente or just propaganda games remains an open question. In practical terms the most tangible outcome was the Austrian State Treaty of 1955, which secured the withdrawal of all foreign occupation troops and the re-establishment of Austria (which had been taken over by Nazi Germany in 1938) as an independent but neutral state.

Meanwhile, the process of consolidating the cold war blocs in Europe continued apace. The early 1950s was a period of massive rearmament on both sides of the iron curtain (the Red Army, for example, doubled in size between 1948 and 1953), and of the dawn of the thermonuclear age as both the United States and the Soviet Union tested H-bombs hundreds of times more powerful than the A-bombs which had been dropped by the Americans on Hiroshima and Nagasaki in 1945. In May 1955, a rearmed West Germany was admitted to NATO; in response Moscow set up the Warsaw Pact, including East Germany as a member. But even as Europe definitively split into two heavily armed nuclear camps, the political atmosphere was far less tense and east–west

relations far more stable than at the height of the cold war confrontation a few years earlier.

This first postwar decade of Soviet foreign policy overlapped with the
final years of the Stalin regime. After the Second World War the Soviet
dictator, who died in March 1953, maintained an iron grip on Soviet
foreign policy. In later years Soviet foreign policy became subject to
more regularised and collective control by the Soviet leadership and
more open to the influence of a variety of party, state and policy advice
bodies. Under Stalin, however, foreign policy decision-making was
highly centralised and personalised. Soviet foreign policy in the postwar
years was very much Stalin's policy. A good definition of the character
of Stalin's foreign policy is that it was

> messianic in its world view, limited in its geographical and functional
> scope, pessimistic in its evaluation of situations, parsimonious in its
> acceptance of costs and risks.
>
> (article by Roberts 1994, p. 1386, n. 66)

Stalin, it could be said, was a careful ideologue, who conducted a radically inclined but conservatively calculated foreign policy. The same
combination of zeal and caution (but with more bluster) was also characteristic of Molotov, Soviet Foreign Minister from 1939 to 1949, and
Stalin's closest collaborator on foreign policy matters. During the war
these two had controlled Soviet foreign policy as if it were a personal
fiefdom. This duopoly of foreign policy decision-making continued
after the war and together they shaped the Soviet response to the challenge of peace.

SOVIET PEACE AIMS AND THE GRAND ALLIANCE, 1945–7

Soviet peace aims had emerged gradually in the period 1943–5 during
the course of complex discussions and negotiations within the wartime
coalition and in the context of a variety of changing pressures, influ-
ences, and circumstances. Hence, the coherence of the resultant policy
programme should not be overestimated. In so far as there was a Soviet
plan for the postwar world it was (in its most benign form) a programme for peace, security and socialist progress. These goals were to
be achieved by

1 the maintenance of allied unity after the war
2 the prevention of a resurgence of German power
3 the establishment of a Soviet sphere of influence in eastern Europe

4 the transformation of Europe into a region of 'new' or 'people's' democracy
5 the assertion of the USSR's great power status, rights and interests
6 the postwar repair and reconstruction of the Soviet economy and the resumption of the building of socialism in the USSR.

The first and second of these policies were intimately linked. One of Moscow's main incentives for the continuation of the Grand Alliance was to ensure that never again would Germany threaten war and aggression against the USSR, or any other country for that matter. Germany had waged a war of annihilation against the USSR and Stalin was determined to annihilate permanently German power and the German threat. That goal, the Soviet leader felt, required long-term co-operation with Britain and the United States over the joint occupation and joint repression of Germany.

There were other incentives to maintain postwar allied unity. Moscow was tempted by President Roosevelt's wartime idea of the Big Three as a global police force, working together within the United Nations to impose peace and order on the world. Moscow also feared that the alternative to allied unity and co-operation was a division of the world into hostile and competing blocs; in particular, the emergence of a western bloc antagonistic to the USSR. Finally, there were also economic incentives (very important given the extent of Soviet war damage: between 20 million and 30 million war dead; 70,000 cities, towns and villages laid waste; thousands of miles of roads and railway track destroyed; industry and agriculture in European Russia utterly devastated). The Soviets needed British and American co-operation to secure reparations from German industry, which was mainly located in the western-occupied zones of Germany. It was also possible that American loans and grants could be made to aid Soviet reconstruction. More generally, this was a time when Soviet participation in a new world economic order was under consideration in Moscow. Such a radical break with traditional Soviet economic isolationism was conceivable only in the framework of a friendly and stable new world political order.

The second main prong of Moscow's peace programme was a series of unilateral measures to strengthen Soviet security. The key policy was the creation of a Soviet sphere of influence in eastern Europe. Such a 'sphere of influence' was defined as a zone of Soviet strategic and foreign policy domination, an area within which Moscow would brook no interference by any other great power. What that meant in practical terms was the establishment of a series of friendly, pro-Moscow regimes in Albania, Bulgaria, Czechoslovakia, Finland, Hungary, Poland,

Romania and Yugoslavia, with the aim of ensuring that never again would eastern Europe act as a bridgehead for an invasion of the USSR as it had done for Germany in June 1941. Never again would east European states be ruled by hostile, anti-Soviet governments; in some cases governments so hostile that they had joined in the German attack on Russia. This was true of Finland, Hungary and Romania. (Even traditionally pro-Russian Bulgaria had been a Germany ally in the Second World War, although it had not declared war on the Soviet Union.)

Because of the military situation at the end of the war – the Red Army occupied virtually the whole of eastern Europe – Moscow had the power to impose its will on the region. The Soviet position in eastern Europe was also buttressed by a number of wartime agreements with Britain and the United States which gave the Red Army political control over the occupation regimes in Bulgaria, Finland, Hungary and Romania (just like the British and Americans had in Italy). The growing strength of the east European communist parties also helped. With the support and sponsorship of Moscow, in 1944–6 these parties rapidly grew into mass political movements. Levels of popular support ranged from an estimated 20–25 per cent in Hungary through to the majority commanded by the communists and their collaborators in Czechoslovakia and Yugoslavia. At the end of the war, anti-fascist coalition governments had assumed power throughout eastern Europe. The strong presence in these new governments of the communists and their allies acted as a guarantee of their continuing fealty to Moscow.

Although driven by defence and security calculations, there were also important political and ideological dimensions to the Soviet project of creating a sphere of influence in eastern Europe. The Soviet and communist aim in eastern Europe was not only to exercise control over foreign policy, but also to create a new social and political order in each country: what the communists called 'new democracy' or, more commonly, 'people's democracy'. In later years, after the outbreak of the cold war, people's democracy became little more than a synonym for Soviet-style socialism and communist party rule. But in the early postwar years the concept had different connotations. It referred to progressive regimes of the political left committed to egalitarian economic and social reform and to regimes governed by genuine multi-party coalitions in which the communists played a leading but not necessarily dominating role. The Soviet sphere of influence in eastern Europe was to be a political space of security as well as a military one, occupied in the long term not by the Red Army but by regimes of people's democracy.

The policy and practice of people's democracy was not limited to eastern Europe. It was the communist project in western Europe, too. The upsurge in popular support for the communist parties was a continent-wide phenomenon. Communist participation in postwar coalition governments was the norm in western Europe as well as eastern Europe. In France and Italy, the mass communist parties which emerged from the wartime resistance movements were in government and were significant players in their countries' postwar politics.

The policy of the west European communists was broadly similar to that of their eastern comrades: anti-fascist national unity; economic reconstruction and modernisation; social reform; centre-left coalition politics; and, of course, foreign policy support for the Soviet Union. Stalin was a key figure in encouraging such a restrained political course – in eastern as well as western Europe. Time and again Stalin reined in the militant tendencies of the communist movement and urged a relatively moderate course of political action on the leaders of the European communist parties. Togliatti, the leader of the Italian communists, was advised by Stalin to enter a government of national unity in Italy led by an ex-fascist general. Stalin told the Hungarian communists that they would have to wait 10 to 15 years before assuming complete power. In conversations with Yugoslav comrades he mused on the possibilities of a socialist Britain under the monarchy. Mao Zedong and the Chinese communists were advised to enter into a postwar alliance with their arch-enemies, Chiang Kai-shek's nationalists. In September 1946, Stalin told the Bulgarian communists that they should form a broad-based 'Labour' party and pursue a 'minimalist programme'.

Stalin's 'moderation' was partly a matter of political expediency. Communist disavowal of revolution, especially in western Europe, was part of the price to be paid for a continuing alliance with capitalist Britain and the United States. But it was also based on a (temporary, it turned out) ideological conversion to the view that socialism in Europe would be achieved gradually, over a long period of time, and on the basis of specific national particularities and peculiarities. In this view, the next stage on the road to socialism in Europe was the democratic reform of capitalism, not its revolutionary overthrow.

From Moscow's point of view the dual project of people's democracy and a Soviet–eastern European security bloc was compatible with the continuation of the Grand Alliance. People's democracy was seen as a social and political transitional form of state which posed no immediate threat to the continued existence of capitalism. Indeed, what the communists were trying to achieve in eastern Europe was not radically different from what had happened to capitalism in Britain, the United States and other countries. As result of the war governments had come to play a more active role in the regulation of the capitalist economy and had allowed the working class and the labour movement a greater share of political power. Postwar Britain was ruled by a Labour government committed to extensive nationalisation of basic industries – coal, steel, gas, etc. – and to radical welfare reform. In the United States, the progressive New Deal coalition of the Roosevelt era still seemed to hold sway (although FDR himself had died in April 1945). In both countries there were 'reactionary' groups advocating anti-communist and anti-Soviet policies. But there were also 'progressives' urging a continuation of the alliance with Russia. The outcome of the struggle between these two political trends was by no means certain, but in 1945–6 the tide of history still seemed to be running strongly in Moscow's favour.

The Soviet insistence on friendly governments in eastern Europe was seen by Moscow as a legitimate security demand that posed no threat to the west. Moscow was, moreover, prepared to concede to the British and Americans their own sphere(s) of influence in western Europe, and in other parts of the globe. The Soviets were concerned about the dangers of a postwar division of the world into opposing blocs, but were not hostile to geopolitical blocs *per se*, only antagonistic ones which could threaten Soviet interests. Indeed, one strand of Soviet thinking suggested that the basis for the continuation of the Grand Alliance should precisely be the division of the world into American, British and Russian spheres of influence. That way conflicts between the allies could be minimised by a clear demarcation of interests. Such thinking was shared by some western officials, but it was not very practical policy since the British and especially US governments denied any interest in concluding such a grand spheres of influence arrangement. Soviet concessions to western security concerns, therefore, took a more *ad-hoc* form. Stalin's refusal to intervene on behalf of the communist side in the Greek civil war was one example – Greece having long been conceded to a British sphere of influence in the Mediterranean.

A peacetime Grand Alliance, a people's democratic Europe, a demarcation of Soviet and western interests – this was Moscow's alternative to what later became known as the cold war. But the political feasibility of the Soviet alternative to the cold war depended on the western perception of and response to Moscow's foreign policy. One problem was that Soviet foreign ambitions were not limited to a sphere of influence in eastern Europe. Moscow had other demands to make as well. In the Far East, Stalin wanted a share of the postwar occupation of Japan. In the Middle East, he wanted Iranian oil concessions and a sphere of influence in the north of the country. In the Near East he wanted control of the Black Sea Straits. In the Mediterranean he wanted the trusteeship of the former Italian colony of Tripolitania (i.e. western Libya).

There were obvious economic and strategic reasons for each of these demands, but they reflected, too, the 'great power' mentality which gripped Stalin and Molotov after the war. These demands were seen as the USSR's entitlements as a victor state and as a great power. Such demands may also have been seen as possible elements of a grand post-war deal with the British and Americans. But London and Washington had other ideas and firmly resisted all these attempted Soviet encroachments in areas of western interest. In each case Moscow backed off because it could not force its wishes on the British and Americans and none of the demands was seen as worth the break up of the Grand Alliance.

In London and Washington, however, it was not the Soviet retreat which grabbed the attention, but the initial demands, which were viewed as expressions of Soviet expansionist tendencies. The British and Americans applied the same reasoning to eastern Europe. What mattered was not the limits of Soviet ambitions, but the exclusion of western influence from the region. What mattered to the Foreign Office and the State Department was not the theory of people's democracy, but the extent of communist control and the rough-house, anti-democratic politics practised by the communist parties, especially in Bulgaria, Poland, Romania and Yugoslavia. (In Czechoslovakia, Finland, and Hungary the communists were, by western standards, better behaved, at least for a time.)

Not that the British and Americans could do anything about Soviet and communist activities in eastern Europe except protest, loudly and frequently. What they could do was to resist what they saw as further communist subversion and Soviet expansion in Europe, to stop what one British official called the USSR's 'ideological lebensraum'. That resistance initially took the form of the Truman Doctrine, the Marshall Plan and the division of Germany. To Moscow these western moves appeared aggressive and threatening, particularly in relation to its strategic-political position in eastern Europe. The Soviet leadership responded in kind, issuing a clarion call for resistance to capitalist and imperialist threats and encroachments. The cold war had started.

OUTBREAK AND DEVELOPMENT OF THE COLD WAR, 1947–50

Dating the origins of the cold war is a much debated subject. Some historians argue that the cold war began with western opposition to the

Bolshevik takeover of Russia in 1917. Others focus on difficulties and conflicts within the wartime Grand Alliance. Another school of thought emphasises the threatening impact of the American A-bombing of Hiroshima and Nagasaki in 1945 – an act aimed as much at intimidating Moscow as ending the war with Japan. Much less contentious is the date of the 'declaration' of the cold war. Many would argue for Churchill's 'iron curtain' speech of March 1946, but most would plump for President Harry S. Truman's speech to the US Congress on 12 March 1947:

> The peoples of a number of countries . . . have recently had totalitarian regimes forced upon them against their will. The Government of the United States has made frequent protests against coercion and intimidation . . . in Poland, Romania, and Bulgaria. I must state also that in a number of other countries there have been similar developments. At the present moment in world history nearly every nation must choose between alternative ways of life. . . . One way of life is based on the will of the majority, and is distinguished by free institutions, representative government, free elections, guarantees of individual liberty, freedom of speech and religion and freedom from political oppression. The second way of life is based upon the will of a minority forcibly imposed upon the majority. It relies upon terror and oppression, a controlled press and radio, fixed elections and the suppression of personal freedoms. I believe it must be the policy of the United States to support free peoples who are resisting attempted subjugation by armed minorities or by outside pressures. I believe that we must assist free peoples to work out their own destinies in their own way. . . . The world is not static, and the status quo is not sacred. But we cannot allow changes in the status quo . . . by such methods as coercion, or by such subterfuges as political infiltration.

The ostensible purpose of Truman's speech was to persuade Congress to vote financial aid for the Greek and Turkish governments (both seen to be under subversive/coercive threat). Although neither the Soviets nor the communists were even mentioned in the speech, there was no doubting the targets of Truman's missive: communist subversion and Soviet coercion, especially in eastern Europe. What Truman said in the quoted passage later became known as the Truman Doctrine: the doctrine of the global defence of the free world against communism. One of the means by which this doctrine would be implemented was the policy of containment, i.e. the containment of Soviet expansionism by the deployment of countervailing power. What the containment concept represented was a growing consensus among US foreign policy decision-makers that the USSR was not a state that you could negotiate or bargain with diplomatically and politically. The language of power and force, it was argued, was the only discourse Soviet leaders understood and responded to.

The initial Soviet response to the Truman Doctrine was surprisingly subdued. Soviet newspapers carried articles and reports critical of Truman's speech, but there was no official counterblast. Soviet foreign policy attention in spring 1947 was focused not on Washington but on Moscow, where a foreign ministers' conference (involving Britain, France, the US and the USSR) had recently opened. The subject of the conference was the future of Austria and Germany. Throughout the six weeks of the conference (a long duration for such a gathering, even in those days) the Soviets attempted – unsuccessfully – to pursue what they considered to be a collaborative agenda on the German question. Despite the impasse reached at the conference, Stalin's assessment was still positive: an allied compromise on Germany was, he said, in reach on all the important issues such as 'democratisation, political organisation, economic unity and reparations'.

Herein lies, perhaps, the clue to Soviet passivity in the face of Truman's declaration of the cold war. Stalin himself was still wedded to the perspective of coexistence and co-operation with the west. It was the view he had propounded in a series of public statements in 1946 and which he repeated in the aftermath of the foreign ministers' conference, including in his interview in May 1947 with Senator Stassen that was quoted earlier (p. 14).

The Soviet response to the Truman Doctrine was not long in coming, however. The event which precipitated it was the Marshall Plan. It was in the light of the Marshall Plan that Moscow began to take the Truman Doctrine more seriously and to link the two together in the perception of an American project of constructing an anti-Soviet western bloc in Europe.

What later became the European Recovery Programme (ERP), colloquially known as the Marshall Plan, was an American financial aid programme for Europe, first proposed by the US Secretary of State George C. Marshall in a speech at Harvard University on 5 June 1947. What Marshall and the Americans had in mind was financial aid for western Europe which, because of its dire postwar economic conditions, was seen as being under threat of a communist takeover. But neither eastern Europe nor the Soviet Union was excluded from receiving assistance from the projected aid package. Indeed, at the end of June, Molotov met with Bevin and Bidault, his British and French foreign minister counterparts, in Paris to discuss a common European response to Marshall's speech.

The Soviets approached the Paris conference in two minds. On the one hand, the Marshall Plan was seen as a device to establish American economic domination of Europe and part of the developing scenario of creating an anti-Soviet western bloc. On the other hand, they saw American financial aid to Europe as a means of staving off a postwar economic depression in the United States. That suggested the possibility of an economic quid pro quo involving the Soviet Union and eastern Europe: America would aid European (and Soviet) recovery which would in turn provide a market for American exports and investments.

Molotov went to Paris to find out from the Americans' British and French allies what the Marshall Plan was all about. What he found were proposals for a co-ordinated European recovery programme, involving multilateral (i.e. regional) agreements, institutions and procedures. Moscow saw that as opening the door to western interference in the affairs of its sphere of influence in eastern Europe. Molotov countered with proposals for a series of bilateral (i.e. country-to-country) financial assistance agreements with the Americans. When these were rejected the discussions with the British and French in Paris came to an end.

In his final statement to the conference on 2 July 1947 Molotov denounced the Marshall Plan as an attempt to undermine the sovereignty and independence of European states and as the harbinger of a divided Europe. Subsequently, the USSR and its east European allies refused to participate in any further discussions about the Marshall Plan. Instead, Moscow launched the so-called Molotov Plan – a series of bilateral trade treaties between the Soviet Union and eastern Europe. Later, in 1949, the Soviets set up the Council for Mutual Economic Assistance (CMEA or Comecon) – a sort of communist alternative to the ERP.

The Marshall Plan finally convinced Moscow that a peacetime alliance with the west was no longer an option. Stalin moved to counter the emerging anti-Soviet western bloc. First came a Soviet riposte to the Truman Doctrine – which took the form of an ideological counter-declaration of the cold war. Then came the consolidation of Soviet and communist power in eastern Europe, followed, in 1948–9, by a confrontation with the west over the future of Germany. With the outbreak of the Korean War in 1950 the cold war contest spilled over into the Far East.

The Soviet counterpart to the Truman Doctrine was the so-called 'two-camps' doctrine propounded in a speech by Politburo member

A.A. Zhdanov at the end of September 1947. Zhdanov was a prominent member of the Soviet party leadership who had special responsibility for questions of ideology, foreign policy and communist movement affairs. His speech 'On the international situation' was written in close consultation with Stalin.

The forum for Zhdanov's speech was the first conference of the Communist Information Bureau (Cominform). The Cominform was a sort of successor to the Communist International (or Comintern) which had been abolished by Stalin in 1943. Like its predecessor, Cominform was a formal structure for the exercise of Soviet ideological direction and control of the international communist movement. But unlike the Comintern, the Cominform did not involve all the world's communist parties. Although the Cominform laid down the political line to be adopted by all communists, its conferences and meetings were attended only by representatives of the Soviet, Bulgarian, Czechoslovakian, French, Hungarian, Italian, Polish, Romanian and Yugoslavian communist parties, that is the governing parties of eastern Europe plus the two largest communist parties in western Europe. Notable absentees included the German communists, who by this time ruled the Russian zone of occupation in Eastern Germany; the Greek communists, who were still fighting the civil war that had broken out when the country was liberated from Nazi occupation in 1944; and the Finnish communist party – a very large party, which unlike those of their French and Italian comrades was still at this time a member of the nation's governing coalition. Neither were the Chinese communists – about to take power in their country – invited. Cominform was a strictly European affair.

The precise origins of Moscow's decision to establish the Cominform are not entirely clear. It seems that the idea of a successor to Comintern had been in the air since the end of the war, and not only in Moscow. The Yugoslav communists were particularly keen on the establishment of a new international communist organisation which would enable them to push for the adoption of a more militant and revolutionary line by some of their brother parties. For their part, the Soviets wanted to rein in the activities of foreign communist parties, particularly those with independent power and prestige. Moscow felt that it had, at the very least, the right to be consulted on all major decisions. In this connection, Moscow was not amused by the failure of the French and Italian communist parties to keep them informed about the events leading to both parties' expulsion from their national governing coalitions in May 1947. This was one reason for the involvement of these two parties in the Cominform. Indeed, at the first Cominform conference the major topic of discussion was criticism of the 'reformist policies' and 'parliamentary illusions' of the French and Italian communists.

The final decision to go ahead with the Cominform was made at around the same time as the breakdown of Soviet–western negotiations about the Marshall Plan. The extent to which the establishment of Cominform was a direct response to the Truman Doctrine and the Marshall Plan remains unclear. What is certain is that Soviet preparations for the Cominform conference became intimately bound up with a fundamental reassessment of the international situation in the light of developments augured by the Truman Doctrine and the Marshall Plan. When Zhdanov spoke at the Cominform conference he unveiled both a new political line for the communist movement and a radical turn in Soviet foreign policy.

In his speech Zhdanov proclaimed that the world had divided into two camps: an anti-imperialist and democratic camp led by the Soviet Union and an anti-democratic and imperialist camp headed by the United States. Under the guise of the Truman Doctrine and the Marshall Plan an expansionist United States was forming a western bloc with the aim of securing the political and economic enslavement of Europe. On a broader front, the Americans were striving for world domination and preparing to unleash a new war. Standing in the way of these plans and tendencies was, of course, the Soviet Union and its allies, who stood for peace and freedom. (For the speech and the rest of the conference proceedings see Procacci, 1994.)

Following the conference the communist movement executed a 'left turn' in its strategy and policy. In western Europe the communists abandoned the policy of national unity and participation in the postwar reconstruction of their countries'; instead they took on the stance of a militant anti-government opposition, particularly in relation to the Truman Doctrine, the Marshall Plan and US involvement in European affairs. But even in countries where they were still very popular and influential, the capacity of the west European communists to influence the course of events was very limited. Anti-government strikes and protests caused some disruption and added to the growing cold war atmosphere of crisis and tension, but the main achievement of the communist parties was to increase their own political isolation (see the article by Sassoon, 1992).

In eastern Europe, the change in communist policy was much more radical and far-reaching in its effects and consequences. The Cominform conference was the signal for the 'communisation' of the region – the establishment of single-party communist control. As well as securing direct control over all the levers of government, this process typically involved the dissolution and repression of opposition parties, the end of independent left-wing parties by forced socialist-communist party mergers, state control of the press, and increasing communist domination of mass organisations such as the trade unions. This extension of communist political power provided a springboard for the 'sovietisation' of eastern Europe. This meant the imposition of a Soviet model of socialism on eastern Europe: state-owned and controlled economies, centralised planning and direction of the economy, the forced collectivisation of agriculture, and an all-pervasive, dominant communist party presence in social, political and cultural life. There was also an element of 'Stalinisation' in the sense that the regimes tended to be dominated by a single, idolised party leader. Another aspect of the mimicking of the Stalin regime in Russia was the use of political terror – purges, arrests, show trials and executions – to maintain the communist grip on politics and society. Needless to say, the east European regimes were also 'Stalinist' – totally loyal and obedient to the Soviet dictator personally.

The communisation, sovietisation and Stalinisation of eastern Europe did not take place according to a single timetable. Even before the Cominform conference, the process of transforming people's democracy into full-blown communist regimes was far advanced in several countries (Yugoslavia, Bulgaria and Romania), while in others (Poland, Hungary and East Germany) there were already distinct tendencies in that direction. In Czechoslovakia coalitionist people's democracy lasted until a government crisis in February 1948 which resulted in the ousting from power of liberal and centre parties. In Finland, too, there was a government crisis (in summer 1948) which brought to an end the people's democratic experiment, but this time it was the communists that found themselves outside the cabinet and in opposition. But Moscow was prepared to accept that outcome provided the Finns pursued a friendly foreign policy towards the USSR. (On Finland see the articles by Korobochkin, 1995 and Nevakivi, 1994.)

The communist takeover in eastern Europe had a local (i.e. country-specific) timetable as well as that related to Soviet foreign policy and the outbreak of the cold war. East European communists had their own ideas about policy and strategy, often more militant and radical than those proposed by Moscow. Indeed, a major problem for the early post-war Soviet concept of creating a relatively liberal regime of people's democracy in eastern Europe was the imperfect nature of the main instrument for the achievement of that aim. Except in Czechoslovakia, the communists of eastern Europe had little experience, tradition or personal commitment to democratic politics. Nor were the conditions of wartime devastation, social chaos, ethnic division, economic back-wardness and the widespread practice of political violence conducive to the development of a democratic political culture. Given these factors the east European communist parties were far better suited to the task of establishing dictatorial communist regimes than maintaining people's democratic ones. And it was a task that, for the most part, communist party members as well as their leaders embraced with enthusiasm.

At the forefront of the struggle to implement the new communist line in eastern Europe was the Yugoslav Communist Party (YCP). Under the leadership of Josip Broz Tito the YCP-led partisan movement had liberated Yugoslavia from German occupation largely by its own efforts. The Yugoslav coalition government that emerged at the end of the war was heavily dominated by the communists and, from the very begin-ning, Tito pursued policies aimed at creating a socialist (rather than a people's democratic) Yugoslavia. At the Cominform conference the Yugoslav representatives were in the forefront of the attack on the 'right-wing' policies of the French and Italian communist parties. After the conference the YCP campaigned for the extension of the Yugoslav model of socialism (itself a copy of the Soviet model) to the other people's democratic states. The prestige of the Yugoslav communists – always high because of the partisan struggle – was further enhanced by the decision that the headquarters of the new Communist Information Buro would be in Belgrade. The scene seemed set for the consolidation of Tito and YCP's status as the number two party in the world com-munist movement. In March 1948, however, there developed a split between Moscow and Belgrade and by the time of the second Cominform Conference in June 1948 the YCP had been expelled from the communist movement.

The cause of the Stalin–Tito split was Yugoslav resistance to Soviet leadership and control of the emerging communist bloc. However, the circumstances of the initial schism were to say the least somewhat iron-ical. Tito's resistance to Moscow was, it seems, precipitated by Soviet opposition to Yugoslav designs on Albania and Bulgaria. Stalin had no objection in principle to Yugoslav plans to dominate Albania, but he insisted on the careful and gradual implementation of such plans. Nor was Stalin opposed to the establishment of a Yugoslav–Bulgarian fed-eration or confederation, but not one dominated by Belgrade or one which could become a base for Yugoslavian leadership of a Balkan bloc. Stalin was also concerned to avoid actions in eastern Europe that would be overly provocative to the west.

At stake in the Soviet–Yugoslav dispute was Moscow's claim to lead-ership of the communist camp, including the right of consultation and veto on all major questions of foreign policy. That kind of leadership and direction the Yugoslav communists were not prepared to accept. They saw it as the assertion of Soviet national interests over their own and decided to assert their right – as communists and as leaders of a sovereign state – to differ politically with Moscow. It was not a challenge that Stalin was prepared to countenance. Tito and the YCP leadership were denounced as traitors to the communist movement and excommunicated. As the dispute escalated so did the accusations of treason. At its climax in the early 1950s the Titoites were characterised as imperialist agents carrying out a restoration of capitalism in Yugoslavia. In the hunt for Titoite heretics and pro-capitalist conspirators elsewhere, the east European communist parties were hit by a wave of purges and treason trials. The victims included many prominent party and government officials. In the Czechoslovak 'show trial' of 1952 the star accused was none other than the party's former General Secretary, Rudolf Slansky. Slansky was one of 14 high-ranking party members at this trial who publicly confessed their anti-socialist treachery. All were convicted and 11, including Slansky, were executed. (All the defendants were subsequently 'rehabilitated', i.e. deemed to be loyal communists who had been victims of a Stalinist frame-up.)

Not until 1956 was the Soviet–Yugoslav relationship fully restored, at which point Moscow's earlier accusations against the YCP were repudiated. Tito, however, continued to keep his distance from Moscow, maintaining Yugoslavia's position of non-alignment in the cold war adopted after its expulsion from the Soviet bloc. (On the Stalin–Tito dispute see Gibianskii, 1998 and other articles by the same author.)

The Soviet–Yugoslav split had a decisive effect on the character of the communist bloc which emerged in the late 1940s and early 1950s. Was the bloc to be a Soviet-led alliance or was it to be a Moscow-dominated monolith in which there would be no deviation from the Soviet line on ideology, politics or foreign policy? The Stalin–Tito conflict settled the issue very definitely in favour of no deviation. That, however, was only the theory. In practice, the Yugoslav challenge to Soviet leadership and control of the communist bloc was the first of many east European deviations from the Moscow line. In Hungary in 1956, internal political convulsions within the communist party sparked off a popular revolt against communist rule and Soviet domination. In 1960, Albania sided with China in the Sino-Soviet dispute. In the mid-1960s Romania adopted a series of domestic and foreign policies designed to assert its difference and autonomy from the rest of the Soviet bloc. In 1968, an attempt by the leadership of the Czechoslovak communist party to replace Soviet-style socialism with a more liberal, home-grown version was crushed by Soviet tanks. In the 1970s and 1980s the communist regime in Poland was challenged, and eventually undermined, by the independent workers' movement Solidarity. From the 1940s through to the 1980s the Soviet and communist position in eastern Europe was fragile and unstable.

THE GERMAN QUESTION

While the consolidation of communist power in eastern Europe was one element of the Soviet cold war counter-offensive to the Truman Doctrine and the Marshall Plan, another was a more aggressive approach to the German question. The most dramatic act here was the Soviet imposition in June 1948 of a blockade, cutting road and rail links between West Germany and West Berlin. In response the western allies launched the famous Berlin airlift, supplying by air the American, British and French occupied sectors of the German capital.

The Berlin blockade crisis arose out of the breakdown in the early postwar period of Soviet–western negotiations about the future of Germany. During the war it had been agreed that, following its defeat, Germany would be divided into American, British, French and Soviet zones of military occupation. Berlin, which lay deep inside the Soviet zone of occupation in East Germany, would – for symbolic and political reasons – also be so divided. Each country would control its own zone and sector of Berlin, but there would also be an Allied Control Council (ACC) which would co-ordinate the implementation of common policies on the demilitarisation, denazification and democratisation of Germany as a whole. In general terms the shared perspective of the Grand Alliance partners was that the danger of a postwar revival of German aggression would be dealt with by joint occupation and by a long-term, permanent diminution of German power.

Wartime agreements on occupation zones and the establishment of the ACC were readily implemented, as were various decisions on changes to Germany's prewar territorial boundaries, including the transfer of East Prussian territory to Poland and the return of the Sudetenland (occupied by Germany following the Munich agreement of 1938) to Czechoslovakia. Within each zone various measures of demilitarisation, denazification and democratisation were also carried out. The problem area was the question of the long-term future and character of the postwar German state, particularly what would happen to the country when the allied military occupation ended. During the war neither the western powers nor the USSR were entirely clear about what they wanted in this respect, but in the early postwar years there quickly developed a fundamental divergence between Soviet and western aims concerning the future of Germany.

Stalin's aim for postwar Germany was a variation of the more general project of a people's democratic Europe. Postwar Germany would, ideally, be a left-wing, democratic and anti-fascist state ruled by the communists and their allies. This was the policy pursued and implemented in the Soviet zone of occupation, with the perspective of extending the people's democracy model to the rest of the country in due course. At the same time, Stalin had economic aims in Germany – the extraction of reparations (mainly in the form of capital equipment and industrial goods) to aid Russia's postwar reconstruction. However, the latter goal tended to conflict with Soviet political aims in Germany: Soviet economic pillage of their zone of occupation did little to endear the local communists to the German people.

Reparations were also a source of tension in Soviet–western relations in occupied Germany. The western powers resisted Soviet demands for reparations from the zones they occupied. The reparations imposed on Germany after the First World War had been a political and financial disaster, it was argued by the British and Americans. Indeed, reparations had contributed to the destabilisation of Germany that had brought Hitler and the Nazis to power. Reparations would do no one any good and would compound Germany's dire economic situation, or so the British and Americans thought. The western aim was, therefore, a German economic revival as part of a wider postwar European economic recovery. Neither did the west have any intention of allowing a united Germany to fall under communist and Soviet sway. Hence, there was a general drift in postwar western policy towards a political and economic division of Germany. After the outbreak of the cold war this orientation toward a division of Germany took on a much more definite and explicit form. In effect, Germany was where the western powers chose to take a stand against further Soviet and communist encroachments in Europe.

At the end of 1947 Soviet–western negotiations about the future of Germany broke down completely. In early 1948 the western powers announced plans which signalled their intention to establish a separate west German state. One of those policies was the introduction of a new currency in the western zone of occupation – thereby furthering the economic division of the country. It was ostensibly in protest at the western currency reform that the Soviet Union launched its land blockade of Berlin. However, the real Soviet target was the projected West German state and its integration into a western cold war bloc. The blockade was essentially a negotiating tactic designed to avert that integration and to pressurise the western powers into further negotiations about the future of Germany. The tactic backfired badly on the Russians. Not only were the western allies able to keep West Berlin supplied by air and to stonewall Soviet demands for further negotiations, but also they scored a major propaganda victory when in May 1949 the Russians backed down and lifted the blockade. That same month saw the establishment of the (West) German Federal Republic (FRG). In October 1949 the Soviets countered with the transformation of their zone of occupation into the (East) German Democratic Republic (GDR). But the division of Germany was, from the Soviet point of view, far from being an ideal solution to the German question. In April 1949 the NATO alliance treaty was signed. West Germany was not a signatory, but there was no doubting the new state's alignment with NATO and with the western bloc that Moscow so feared, which now had a formalised military-political existence.

The Soviet blockade of Berlin was a major act of provocation, but it was not intended to provoke an overly aggressive western response. Moscow's calculation was that the western response to the blockade would be restrained and that the Soviet offer of further negotiations on Germany would be accepted with alacrity. The Soviets miscalculated the western response but no dire consequences for the USSR flowed from this mistake. The same could not be said of Stalin's next error of judgement – which resulted in the outbreak of a war in Korea which lasted three years, cost up to 10 million casualties, and at times threatened to expand from a limited, local war to a more general, perhaps even global nuclear, conflict.

THE KOREAN WAR

Not surprisingly, the outbreak of the Korean War in June 1950 is an event which has attracted a lot of attention from historians. In the post-cold war era, interest has been further fuelled by the accessing of many new documents from Russian, Chinese and Korean archives. Perhaps the most important finding from the new evidence is that the main architect of the outbreak of the war was Kim Il Sung, the North Korean communist leader. It was Kim who proposed to Stalin a North Korean invasion of South Korea with the aim of establishing a unitary communist regime for the whole country. It was Kim who convinced Stalin that unification of Korea by force was militarily and politically feasible.

Until 1945 Korea was a Japanese colony. When Japan surrendered in August 1945, Russian and American forces moved into Korea and the country was divided along the thirty-eighth parallel into Russian and American zones of occupation. Russian and American troops evacuated Korea in 1948–9 but they left behind them two governments-cum-states: an authoritarian communist regime in the North headed by Kim Il Sung and an authoritarian capitalist regime in the South headed by Syngman Rhee. Both Kim and Rhee had ambitions to extend their rule to the whole country and in the period before the war there was much sabre-rattling by both sides and numerous small-scale military engagements along the border.

In the event it was Kim who struck first. On 25 June 1950 the North Koreans launched a full-scale military invasion of the South. The attack was launched with Stalin's full blessing, indeed the military plan of campaign had been drawn up by the Soviet military. Initially, the North Korean invasion was highly successful. By the end of the summer virtually the whole of South Korea was in communist hands. In the meantime, however, the United States had mobilised a UN-endorsed coalition in support of South Korea. In September the American-led forces launched a series of successful counter-offensives. Now it was the turn of the North Koreans to retreat as the Americans invaded across the thirty-eighth parallel. Kim's regime was saved from complete defeat only by large-scale Chinese intervention on his behalf. So-called Chinese 'volunteers' drove the UN forces out of North Korea and the South found itself once more under threat of communist invasion. However, the contest soon stalemated into a struggle of attrition along the thirty-eighth parallel. In July 1951 armistice negotiations began which, after two years of talks, resulted in an end to the war in July 1953. Both the Kim and the Rhee regimes survived the war, as did the thirty-eighth parallel border between North Korea and South Korea.

From the point of view of the analysis of postwar Soviet foreign policy, one of the key questions about the Korean War must be the circumstances and motives of Stalin's decision to give the green light to Kim Il Sung's invasion.

At the time the North Korean invasion of the South was perceived by many western politicians and decision-makers as a covert act of *Soviet* aggression. North Korea was seen as a Soviet client state and Kim as acting on Stalin's orders. The war in Korea was seen as part of a pattern of Soviet-sponsored communist aggression and expansionism which threatened further encroachments on the 'free world' if South Korea was not defended. As with many other aspects of the cold war conflict, the truth was much more complex and contradictory.

It was Kim's idea to invade the South. From early 1949 he made repeated proposals to that effect to Stalin and other Soviet representatives. Stalin's initial reaction was to veto such a move and to urge the North Korean comrades to concentrate on supporting the internal struggle (including communist-led guerrilla warfare) within South Korea. Then Stalin shifted to the view that what Kim proposed was acceptable in principle but required a great deal of preparation. Finally, in April 1950 Stalin gave Kim the go-ahead, but only on condition that Mao Zedong and the Chinese comrades endorsed such an action (which, again on Kim's urging, they did shortly after).

Kim's argument in favour of an invasion was that Rhee's regime was rotten and unstable and that a North Korean attack would precipitate a mass revolutionary uprising in the South. What was being proposed, it should be noted, was a revolutionary expansion of socialism in Korea. (Strategic and security calculations figured hardly if at all in the invasion decision.) Crucial to understanding Stalin's endorsement of this perspective is the context of his thinking at this time. As we have seen, there had been a significant expansion of communism in Europe after the Second World War. By the late 1940s, however, it seemed that the revolutionary wave had shifted to the east. All over Asia communist-led national liberation movements were engaged in armed struggles to oust western colonial regimes, most notably in Vietnam. Above all there was the communist victory in the Chinese civil war and the establishment, in October 1949, of the People's Republic of China. The establishment of a communist regime in a united Korea seemed natural and inevitable in such a context. There was, of course, the danger of American intervention in support of South Korea. But the Americans had been prepared to 'lose' much more important China and there were signs that Washington considered Korea to lie outside the US defensive perimeter in East Asia. Stalin may also have calculated that the newly acquired Soviet A-Bomb (the first test was in August 1949) would act as a deterrent against any American counteraction. But perhaps the most important factor tipping the balance in favour of an attack was that Kim offered the prospect of a quick and easy victory which would pre-empt any US involvement in the conflict.

Stalin's decision for war in Korea was an action born out of a sense of confidence and strength. But when it became apparent that he had miscalculated he quickly adopted a more cautious stance. When the American counter-offensive of September–October 1950 threatened the very existence of Kim's regime, there was no question of direct Soviet intervention in his support; that would have been far too provocative and dangerous. The task of saving Kim fell to the Chinese who, at Stalin's urging (and for strategic reasons of their own), sent their 'volunteers' into North Korea on 25 October.

Stalin's decision to back away from a direct confrontation with the United States in Korea obviously had many local and particular reasons (for example, the availability of the Chinese to do the fighting). But it also formed part of an emerging pattern in Soviet foreign policy in the early 1950s: a policy of limiting, de-escalating and stabilising the cold war confrontation with the west.

COEXISTENCE AND THE COLD WAR, 1950–6

While war was raging in Korea, in Europe Moscow was waging a struggle for peace – the first of many Soviet 'peace campaigns' of the cold war era. Soviet 'peace policy' centred on proposals for disarmament, collective security and the neutralisation of Germany. Like all such Soviet campaigns this one in the early 1950s had propaganda, doctrinal and (as Marshall Shulman put it) power-bloc politics aspects (Shulman, 1963 p. 253).

The *propaganda* aspect was Moscow's projection of the USSR as a state that stood for peace in the face of capitalist and imperialist warmongering. There was nothing new in this: the self-definition of the Soviet state as a peace-loving country dated back to 1917 when the new Bolshevik government's very first foreign policy act was to issue a Decree on Peace calling for an end to the First World War. During the interwar years the 'struggle for peace' was one of the great propaganda themes of Soviet foreign policy. This theme re-emerged during the early cold war years with the twofold aim of, on the one hand, blaming the west for the cold war and the war danger and, on the other hand, strengthening the position of Soviet supporters in the capitalist countries who were campaigning against western cold war policies.

It is important to appreciate that to a large extent the Soviet leadership (and the communist party and much of the country) believed its own propaganda. Moscow's politicians really believed that they and their regime stood for the liquidation of the cold war and the inauguration of a new era of peace. Obviously, Moscow's proposals for ending the cold war and the division of Europe were couched in terms that would safeguard and further Soviet political and security interests, but their self-interested character did not make them any less genuine and real – only unacceptable to the west, which had its own ideas about an appropriate basis for ending the cold war conflict.

Soviet self-conceptions of the USSR as a peaceful state were reinforced by the *doctrinal* aspect of Moscow's peace policy. As a matter of doctrine (i.e. of ideology) the Soviets stood for peaceful coexistence between socialism and capitalism. That doctrine was not abandoned when the cold war broke out. Neither did Soviet ideologists ever concede that war between capitalism and socialism was inevitable (or even very likely) – in spite of all their talk about western warmongers, the inherent aggressiveness of capitalism and imperialism, the immediacy of the threat of war, and American preparations for an attack on the USSR, etc. Whether or not the cold war developed into a hot war was seen to depend on the outcome of political struggles at both national and international levels. Peaceful coexistence was a condition that could be forced on the capitalists whether they liked it or not. Such reasoning lay behind the launch of a communist-led world peace movement in 1948–9. This movement campaigned, rallied and petitioned for disarmament and for a reduction of international tensions. At its peak in the early 1950s the movement claimed millions of active supporters across the world. The Stockholm Appeal, a petition calling for the banning of nuclear weapons, launched in the Swedish capital in March 1950, gathered in more than 560 million signatories (Craig Nation, 1992 p. 197).

The existence and activities of the peace movement expressed Soviet concerns about the war danger and Moscow's desire to pressurise western governments to negotiate a relaxation of international tensions, to achieve a détente. This attempt to mobilise public opinion within western countries in support of Soviet peace proposals was a typical tactic of Soviet foreign policy during the cold war.

Two other aspects of Soviet doctrine have a bearing on the thinking behind the 1950s peace campaign. First, there was the belief that because of their competing economic interests the capitalist states were divided among themselves. These 'inter-imperialist contradictions' (for example, between Britain and the US, between Europe and America) – could be diplomatically exploited by the Soviet Union. Second, there was the belief that capitalism was an inherently unstable economic system prone to crises and malfunctioning – a system that would inevitably experience a major economic collapse (and political crisis) in the postwar period.

Within this kind of perspective the western cold war bloc was viewed as (potentially) weak and divided, in contrast to the cohesion and growing strength of the socialist bloc. The prospects for a combined struggle by the USSR, the communist parties and the peace movement in support of Soviet peace policies were seen as far from bleak.

Another aspect of Soviet economic thinking worth mentioning here was the belief in the superiority of the socialist economic system. Stalin believed, as did his successors, that, in the long run, the Soviet command economy was capable of competing effectively with the capitalist economies of the west, indeed of eventually overtaking them. This perception of Soviet and socialist economic strengths reinforced the view that the west could be pressured into peaceful coexistence on Moscow's terms.

The *power-politics* aspect of the Soviet peace campaign was an attempt to disrupt the development of the western cold war bloc. The centrepiece of this strategy was a series of proposals that Germany should be de-occupied, reunited and neutralised, i.e. that Germany (and Austria) would constitute a kind of neutral zone in Europe, aligned with neither side of the cold war divide. These proposals were coupled with others for the establishment of pan-European collective security arrangements involving both west and east European states.

The primary Soviet aim was to detach West Germany from the western alliance, or at least limit its integration into NATO and other western defence arrangements – above all to prevent West German rearmament. The latter development came into prospect in 1950 with the announcement of plans for a European Defence Community which would include West Germany as a member. In response the Soviets proposed new negotiations on the future of Germany as a whole, specifically that there should be a withdrawal of all occupation forces and that the country should be demilitarised.

In March 1952 Moscow issued the first of a series of what historians call the 'Stalin Notes' on Germany. These notes offered, in effect, German unification in exchange for the neutralisation of the country. Despite the west's rejection of this proposal Moscow persisted, making the same offer again at the Soviet–Western foreign ministers' conference in February 1954. Following that conference the Soviets even offered to join NATO themselves. Behind this strange proposal was the concept of a collective security organisation covering the whole of Europe – advocated by Moscow when it became apparent that West Germany was to be rearmed and was going to be admitted to NATO. In May 1955 West Germany joined NATO. A few days later the Soviet Union and its east European allies (including the GDR) signed a multilateral mutual assistance treaty in Warsaw. The signing of the Warsaw Pact constituted the final formalisation of the division of Germany and of Europe into mutually exclusive blocs. But Moscow had still not given up on the idea of pan-European collective security. Article 11 of the Warsaw Pact stated that 'in the event of the organisation of a system of collective security in Europe, and the conclusion of a general European Treaty of collective security . . . the present Treaty shall cease to be effective'.

Were the Soviets serious about cross-bloc collective security? Were they serious about giving up control of East Germany in exchange for German neutrality? The answer to the first question is yes, but Moscow's agenda was the peaceful coexistence and co-operation of the blocs, not their dissolution (and certainly not the dissolution of the Soviet bloc in eastern Europe). But east–west collective security arrangements could contribute to the diminution of cold war tensions and help prevent further polarisation and bloc confrontation in Europe.

Moscow's German policy, the second question, is more difficult to pin down. One answer is that the Soviet proposal for a united but neutral Germany was mostly a tactical, propaganda ploy. Moscow knew that the west would reject its proposals, so there was no harm in making them. Proposing German unity was good domestic politics as far as Soviet supporters within Germany were concerned and German neutrality was an attractive proposition to many NATO members (for example, France, invaded twice by the Germans in the previous 40 years). This interpretation has much logic and evidence on its side. It seems clear that within the Soviet foreign ministry the propagandistic dimension of Soviet proposals on Germany were very much at the forefront of policy thinking. But, as Caroline Kennedy-Pipe (1995) has argued, there was much that was ambivalent about Soviet thinking in relation to Germany. Neutralising the German threat had been a central preoccupation of Soviet foreign policy since the end of the war. It was a goal whose achievement was worth a high price. Did that include giving up communist-controlled East Germany? The answer to that question depended on who you asked and at what point in time. Stalin's preferred solution to that dilemma was, probably, the compromise of a non-socialist but left-leaning united Germany. Others (for example, the leaders of the East German communist party) naturally preferred to emphasise the consolidation of communism in the German Democratic Republic, with the long-term prospect of its extension to the rest of the country.

It seems clear, too, that the workers' revolt in East Germany in June 1953 was a crucial moment in the evolution of Soviet policy on the German question. The need to use the Soviet occupation forces to quell massive protest strikes and demonstrations against the communist government brought home to Moscow the weakness of its political position in a country its loyal supporters had controlled for eight years. And support for the communists in West Germany was weaker still. The prospect of some kind of pro-Soviet Germany, always dim, had faded completely. From that point on Moscow's priority was, increasingly, to shore up the socialist regime in East Germany.

It was unfortunate that the June events in East Germany coincided with leadership succession struggles in Moscow following Stalin's death in March 1953. The loser in that struggle was Beria, the head of the security police, who was arrested and shot in July 1953, following charges that he was planning to establish himself as dictator. Beria was depicted by his opponents in the Soviet leadership as a strong advocate of giving up East Germany in exchange for all-German neutrality. In fact, it seems that Beria's attitudes were part of a policy consensus in Moscow that was drifting in the direction of a radical solution to the German question, but which was blown off course by the June events in the GDR (see the article by Kramer, 1998a). Having denounced Beria for proposing to abandon the East German comrades to their fate, the rest of Soviet leadership found themselves locked into a pro-GDR policy – although that did not stop them from continuing to publicly advocate German reunification. But there was more and more a propagandistic whiff about these Soviet proposals and Moscow's tactics were increasingly negative, that is aimed at disrupting the implementation of western plans for Germany and European security.

At the same time, Moscow's genuine desire to achieve a détente in Europe should not be underestimated. That commitment remained true even if that meant coexisting with a western bloc encamped in West Germany and a NATO armed to the nuclear teeth. This was particularly true of the new, post-Stalin leadership of the Soviet Union.

When Stalin died in March 1953, his place was taken by a collective leadership. The most important members of this collective leadership were Malenkov, the Chairman of the Council of Ministers (i.e. the Soviet prime minister), Khrushchev, the First Secretary of the communist party, Molotov, the Foreign Minister, and Bulganin, the Minister of Defence. Beria, the Minister of Internal Affairs, was also a member of this collective leadership for a short time.

In the domestic sphere the new leadership began to implement a series of policies aimed at the destalinisation and liberalisation of the country, i.e. a softening of the terroristic and dictatorial grip on society and citizens lives characteristic of the previous regime. In the foreign sphere there was a concerted effort to bring about a relaxation of the cold war and to resume the practice of negotiated agreements and compromises with the western powers.

Soviet foreign policy in the early post-Stalin era was closely identified by what was called at the time the 'spirit of Geneva'. This phrase refers to a summit meeting of the leaders of Britain, France, the Soviet Union and the United States held in Switzerland in July 1955 – the first such top-level meeting since the war. In practical terms the summit achieved very little, except a series of decisions to discuss a number of matters further. But the leaders of the four states did meet and talk in a spirit of friendship and they did agree on the need for greater co-operation, rather than more confrontation.

At the summit the Soviets continued to press for a settlement of the German question and for European collective security. They also put forward a series of far-reaching proposals on disarmament and the control of nuclear weapons. Moscow made no headway on these proposals at the summit or at follow-up meetings. But the important thing about Geneva was its sentiments not its substance. The summit, moreover, was not the only important counter-cold war development during this period.

In July 1953 the Korean armistice had been signed. A year later an agreement was reached at an international conference in Geneva on ending the war in Vietnam between French colonial occupying forces and the communist-led National Liberation Front. In May 1955 the USSR and the western powers signed a treaty ending the occupation of Austria and re-establishing the country as an independent and neutral state. In September 1955 the Soviets established diplomatic relations with West Germany. All these acts were practical signs of Moscow's commitment to, where possible, resolving differences with the west and reducing international tensions.

One of the impulses behind Moscow's post-Stalin détente offensive was the revolution in military technology which occurred at this time. In 1952–3 both the United States and the Soviet Union tested thermonuclear devices, H-bombs with enough power to completely destroy even the largest of cities. The development of the cold war into a hot war now threatened death and devastation on a scale many times greater than the Second World War. A third world war could very well turn out to be human civilisation's last act of collective madness.

The Soviet leader most worried about this development was Prime Minister Malenkov. In March 1954 he gave a speech in which he argued that:

> it is not true that humanity is faced with a choice between two alternatives: either a new world war, or the so-called Cold War. The peoples are vitally interested in a durable strengthening of peace. The Soviet government stands for further weakening of international tension, for a stable and durable peace, decisively opposes the Cold War, since that policy is the policy of preparing for a new world war, which with modern weapons means the end of world civilisation.
>
> (Holloway, 1994 p. 336)

Malenkov's view – that atomic war would destroy all human civilisation, capitalist and socialist – reflected the views of many Soviet scientists worried about the H-bomb, but was subsequently repudiated by the rest of the Soviet leadership on the grounds that its emphasis was too fatalistic and pessimistic. Indeed, following criticism of his views at a meeting of the communist party central committee Malenkov was, in February 1955, ousted as Soviet premier. His place was taken by Bulganin, a close collaborator of Khrushchev – the head of the communist party and by now the real power behind the throne.

Khrushchev had joined in the attack on Malenkov, but it was not long before he, too, began to trumpet the dangers of nuclear war. 'Either peaceful coexistence or the most destructive war in history,' he told the twentieth party congress in February 1956. There is no doubt about the sincerity of Khrushchev's anti-war sentiments as stated on this and many other occasions. He, like the rest of the Soviet leadership, had been profoundly influenced by the experience of the Great Patriotic War, in which so many millions of Soviet citizens had died. It is also true that the continued pursuit of peaceful coexistence with the west was the defining feature of Soviet foreign policy during the his period as Soviet leader. But, ironically, the world was never such a dangerous place as during the Khrushchev era. Khrushchev saw nuclear weapons as a threat but he also saw them as an opportunity, a means of securing a 'forced détente'. His nuclear sabre-rattling resulted not in peace but a new era of cold war crisis and confrontation.

3 Coexistence, crisis and schism

The Khrushchev era, 1956–64

Our era [is] an era of Socialist
revolutions and national liberation
revolutions; an era of the collapse of
capitalism and of the liquidation of the
colonial system; and era of the change to
the road to socialism by more and more
nations; and of the triumph of socialism
and communism on a world scale.

(Nikita Khrushchev, January 1961)

OVERVIEW

Nikita Khrushchev's enthronement as Stalin's successor took place in
stages. In September 1953 he was appointed First Secretary of the
Soviet communist party. In February 1955 he was instrumental in forcing Malenkov's resignation as Soviet premier. At the twentieth party
congress in February 1956 – the first such party gathering since the
death of Stalin – Khrushchev was the dominant figure. In June 1957 he
defeated an attempt to depose him by elements of the Stalinist old
guard (including Molotov and Malenkov). Finally, in March 1958
Khrushchev became Chairman of the Council of Ministers (i.e. prime
minister), thus combining the two most powerful positions of the party
and the state.

From the beginning of his reign Khrushchev took an active and vis-
ible interest in foreign affairs: speeches on foreign policy, state visits
abroad, representing the USSR at summits and conferences and in the
forums of international organisations such as the UN. He was involved
in a number of public confrontations with western diplomats and politicians, including a famous occasion at the United Nations in October

1960 when he banged his shoe on the table in order to express his disagreement with what was being said by another delegate!

Behind the scenes Khrushchev was instrumental in all the major Soviet foreign policy decisions. Foreign policy issues, moreover, were central to Khrushchev's disputes and power struggles with other members of the Soviet leadership, particularly Molotov, who opposed Khrushchev's repudiation of many of Stalin's policies.

Like Stalin, Khrushchev stamped Soviet foreign policy with the mark of his own personality. His foreign policy style was exuberant, bombastic and politically and ideologically militant. Content-wise Khrushchev's foreign policy may be characterised as peaceful coexistence with a definite competitive edge. He emphasised peaceful, economic competition between socialism and capitalism, but he projected an equally, if not more, competitive policy in the political, ideological and military spheres.

The Khrushchev era in Soviet foreign policy was punctuated, indeed defined, by a series of diplomatic and political crises: the Soviet invasion of Hungary in 1956, the intense and prolonged Berlin crisis of 1958–61, the beginning in 1960 of the Sino-Soviet split, and the Cuban missile crisis of 1962. All these episodes were intimately bound up with the continuing cold war confrontation with the United States and the west. But perhaps more fundamentally they were all crises of the Soviet bloc, of intra-socialist alliances and relations. Khrushchev ordered the tanks into Budapest to stop the communist regime from being toppled by the people and to avert Hungary's impending departure from the Warsaw Pact. The Berlin crisis was as much about controlling the activities of the East German communist leadership as it was about forcing the negotiation of a western retreat from the German capital. The break with Mao's China was the result of a combination of ideological differences, political-diplomatic conflicts and the breakdown of comradely relations between the Chinese and Soviet communist leaderships. The Cuban missile crisis was provoked by a typically extravagant Khrushchev manoeuvre to prop up and protect the newly fledged socialist regime of Fidel Castro.

The peaceful resolution of what the Soviets called the 'Caribbean Crisis' was followed by a significant reduction of international tensions, signified above all by the Test Ban Treaty of August 1963 which restricted nuclear testing to underground explosions. From the Soviet point of view the 'mini-détente' of the mid-1960s was a resumption of the stabilising and depolarising course charted by the USSR in the early 1950s. However, the confrontation with the United States over Cuba had exposed Soviet strategic nuclear inferiority. The superior

American nuclear arsenal had given Kennedy a definite edge in the brinkmanship of the Cuban missile crisis. The Khrushchev legacy for Soviet foreign policy (he was deposed as leader in October 1964) was an uneasy, dual quest – for détente with the west and for strategic nuclear parity with the United States.

PEACEFUL COEXISTENCE AND NATIONAL LIBERATION

It is conventional to characterise Khrushchev's stewardship of Soviet foreign policy as an era of 'competitive coexistence'. The starting point for this characterisation is Khrushchev's report to the twentieth party congress in February 1956. In his speech Khrushchev reaffirmed the traditional Soviet commitment to a policy of peaceful coexistence, but he also introduced a number of important doctrinal innovations (or, rather, novel emphases). First, he defined peaceful coexistence between the socialist and capitalist systems as a competitive relationship, particularly in the economic sphere: 'we say that the socialist system will win in the competition between the two systems . . . our certainty of the victory of communism is based on the fact that the socialist mode of production possesses decisive advantages over the capitalist mode of production'. (Later, at the twenty-second party congress in 1962, Khrushchev proclaimed the aim of overtaking the United States economically and of completing the building of communism in the USSR by 1980.) Second, Khrushchev revised the Marxist-Leninist precept that war (between capitalist states and between socialist and capitalist states) was inevitable while imperialism existed. He argued that war could be prevented by the political action of the 'peace forces' (communists, socialists and other progressives) who were immeasurably stronger than they had been in the past. Third, Khrushchev argued in favour of the possibility of a peaceful, parliamentary transition to socialism in the advanced capitalist countries. Fourth, Khrushchev noted the development of a new force for peace in world politics: the neutral and non-aligned movement of newly independent countries which had recently thrown off the shackles of colonialism in Asia and Africa.

The strategic thrust of Khrushchev's report was that a major war could be avoided and there could be – indeed there would be – a peaceful, world-wide transition to socialism – certainly a comforting point of view in a world of growing nuclear weaponry. This perspective (which was not without its opponents in the communist movement) was confirmed and elaborated at world communist conferences in 1957 and 1960; at the twenty-first and twenty-second party congresses in 1959 and 1962; and in a growing body of academic and party literature on developments in international relations. Of particular importance was the idea that peaceful, competitive coexistence was a form of class struggle at the international level. Hence, the Soviet pursuit of peaceful coexistence in the cold war was conceived in ideological terms and linked to other (not so peaceful) aspects and forms of class struggle in world politics. At this time the most important of these other forms of class struggle was the anti-colonial and national liberation movement in the so-called 'third world' (the first world being the advanced capitalist states and the second world the socialist bloc). This was the ideological sanction for Moscow's pursuit of an alliance between the socialist bloc and the non-aligned countries of the third world, as well as Soviet support for anti-imperialist movements.

Soviet involvement in 'anti-imperialist struggles' in Asia, Africa and other parts of the world was nothing new, of course. Moscow had always supported and encouraged such national liberation struggles, not least because they were seen as a means of weakening the capitalist-imperialist enemy. Khrushchev continued this tradition but with considerably more emphasis and vigour. This was partly because of the Soviet perception that the focal point for the spread of revolution was now the third world and partly because of greater opportunities for Soviet involvement in third world politics. This was the era of decolonisation and the granting of independence to a large number of former colonial states in Africa, Asia and the Middle East. In many other third world countries violent struggles for national independence were raging. There was also, as R. Craig Nation has pointed out (Craig Nation, 1992 p. 226), a cold war dimension of Moscow's championing of national liberation struggles: an attempt to counter a series of US-sponsored regional security pacts in the Pacific, South East Asia and the Middle East (the ANZUS, SEATO and CENTO treaties of 1951, 1954 and 1955–8, respectively).

The practical face of Soviet policy in the third world was diplomatic support for the Bandung movement of non-aligned states (named after a conference of Asian and African countries held in the Indonesian city in April 1955), economic and military aid to newly independent states (for example, India and Egypt) and political encouragement of the radical tendencies in third world nationalism; the latter effort being informed by the concept that there could be a rapid transition from national liberation to socialism (albeit of a variety different from European socialist systems). Ideologically, Khrushchev trumpeted the justness and legitimacy of 'wars of national liberation'. These wars, he said in 1961, would happen 'as long as imperialism exists, as long as colonialism exists. . . . Such wars are not only admissible but inevitable'. Such rhetoric continued to inform Soviet foreign policy long after Khrushchev was gone. From the very beginning, the Soviet struggle for the third world was as much a political and ideological project as it was a cold war power contest with the United States.

THE POLISH AND HUNGARIAN CRISES OF 1956

At the twentieth congress Khrushchev made another speech which had important implications and ramifications for foreign policy. This was his so-called 'secret speech' denouncing Stalin. At a closed session of the congress on 25 February 1956 Khrushchev criticised Stalin's leadership of the Soviet communist party, repudiated the personality cult surrounding the former Soviet leader, and raged at his mass executions of party and state officials (during the so-called 'Great Terror' of the 1930s). The speech was not officially published, but news of its content quickly leaked (not least because the speech was read out at party meetings all over the Soviet Union).

Khrushchev's purposes in delivering the speech were essentially domestic, part of the continuing campaign of 'destalinisation' and intended to bolster his position against hardline critics of his leadership. At home, it raised hopes and expectations of a fundamental reform of the authoritarian communist system. The same hope persisted in eastern Europe where the secret speech encouraged growing popular dissent and protest, and strengthened the position of reform communists seeking a fundamental change in political direction. The mood for change was furthest advanced in Poland and Hungary.

In Poland matters came to a head when workers rioted in Poznan at the end of June 1956, resulting in hundreds of dead and wounded when Polish security forces opened fire on the demonstrators. The riots had been sparked by opposition to increased work targets, but the protests also had definite political overtones. In response, the Polish United Workers Party (PUWP – the name of the Polish communist party) began moves to restore to power its former leader Gomulka (a victim of the Stalinist purge of so-called 'national communists' in eastern Europe in the late 1940s who was not long out of prison), with a view to implementing a programme of liberalising reform. Moscow, not unnaturally, feared that Gomulka would be too independent and would seek to reduce Soviet influence in Poland.

The crisis point in Polish–Soviet relations was reached when Gomulka met Khrushchev and other Soviet leaders in Warsaw on 19–20 October (they had arrived suddenly in the Polish capital on the very eve of the PUWP central committee meeting that was to elect Gomulka leader). During the talks Khrushchev attempted to browbeat the Poles into moderating their proposed course of action (a key point of contention was the continuing role of the thousands of Soviet advisers and military personnel in Poland attached to the Warsaw government, including the retention by Marshal Konstantin Rokossovky (a Polish-born *Soviet* soldier) of the post of Minister of Defence and commander-in-chief of the Polish armed forces), a posture which was backed up by menacing manoeuvres of Soviet army units stationed in Poland. But Gomulka refused to be intimidated. Faced with the choice between military action and Gomulka's reassurances that neither the communist system in Poland nor the Polish–Soviet alliance was under threat, Khrushchev prudently chose to accept the Pole's word. A Presidium (i.e. Politburo) meeting on 21 October decided to 'refrain from military intervention'. As Khrushchev commented shortly after, 'finding a reason for an armed conflict [with Poland] would be very easy, but finding a way to put an end to such a conflict later would be very hard' (Kramer article, 1996–7 p. 361).

One factor encouraging a peaceful resolution of the Polish crisis was the ominous development of a much more dangerous situation in Hungary. As in Poland, pressure for political change had been growing in Hungary throughout 1956. Indeed, developments in Poland – the Poznan riots, the October crisis – were major encouragements to popular discontent in Hungary. It was a demonstration in Budapest on 23 October in solidarity with the Polish reformers which precipitated the Hungarian crisis. The demonstration (which was illegal) commanded massive popular support and the authorities were unable to control it. Later that day security police opened fire on a breakaway group of demonstrators outside Budapest's main radio station. In response, an armed revolt broke out in the city and the communist government asked for Soviet military assistance to suppress the rebellion. Soviet troops (30,000 of them) intervened the next day, but the fighting escalated in Budapest and other Hungarian cities.

Back in Moscow the Soviet leadership was faced with the choice of intervening in force to quell the revolt and impose order by military might or, as they had done in Poland, to secure a peaceful, political resolution of the crisis. Opinions were divided and there was much wavering in Moscow, but the initial inclination was to give a new Hungarian government headed by the reform communist Imre Nagy a chance to stabilise the situation. But a week later, on 31 October the Presidium decided that the situation was deteriorating rapidly and that military action was necessary. Reports from Soviet representatives in

Hungary indicated that the revolt would have to be crushed by military force. In addition, the Nagy government had embarked on a course which brought it into direct conflict with Moscow; particularly important was Nagy's decision to take Hungary outside of the Warsaw Pact. Given Moscow's recent difficulties with Gomulka and the Poles, a scenario of popular revolts in other communist countries and the collapse of the Soviet–east European bloc was not completely far-fetched. The climax of the Hungarian crisis also coincided with the launch of the Anglo-French attack on Egypt following Nasser's nationalisation of the Suez Canal. At the time a catastrophic Egyptian defeat (Israel attacked as well) seemed inevitable. The loss of Hungary as well as Egypt (one of the USSR's most important third world allies at this time) was too much for Khrushchev to bear. He told the Presidium: 'If we depart from Hungary, it will give a great boost to the Americans, English and French. . . . They will perceive it as weakness on our part and will go onto the offensive. . . . To Egypt [the imperialists] will then add Hungary' (Kramer article, 1996–7 p. 370).

On 4 November the Soviets launched a massive military intervention in Hungary involving the deployment of hundreds of tanks and many tens of thousands of troops. For a few days there was intense fighting on the streets of Budapest and in other towns and cities, resulting in some 25,000 casualties (including 5,000 dead). Following the fighting Moscow installed a new pro-Soviet government headed by Janos Kadar. Among the many victims of the purge that followed was Nagy, who was executed in 1958. Ironically, under Kadar Hungary subsequently evolved into the most liberal and open of the east European communist states. A state much in the image of Nagy's reform communism.

From Moscow's point of view the Hungarian revolt was a 'counter-revolution' which had threatened the overthrow of the country's socialist system, an end to communist control, and the detachment of Hungary from the Soviet bloc. Such an outcome was completely unacceptable to the Soviet leadership. The maintenance of communist control and Soviet domination of eastern Europe remained the defining goal of Moscow's security policy. As Craig Nation points out, that did not mean the Soviets were against change and reform in eastern Europe (Craig Nation, 1992 p. 223). Moscow accepted considerable changes in Poland and in Kadar's Hungary. Nor was Moscow opposed to a degree of national independence in eastern Europe or to a loosening of the reins of Soviet control. At the very height of the Hungarian crisis – on 30 October 1956 – the Soviet government issued a 'Declaration on the Principles of Development and Further Strengthening of Friendship and Cooperation Between the USSR and Other Socialist Countries'.

This appeasing statement promised, in effect, a regularisation of Soviet–east European relations, making them more respectful and equitable than they had been in the past. It was a policy that the Soviets proceeded to implement after the 1956 crisis had passed. Soviet armed forces were withdrawn from a number of east European States. Bilateral and multilateral meetings between the Soviet Union and its east European allies became a regular feature of bloc organisation. Bloc institutions such as the Warsaw Pact and the CMEA developed a genuinely collaborative dimension. Soviet foreign policy, particularly major initiatives in Europe, was conducted more and more in the collective, bloc context. Economic subvention rather than military intervention became the order of the day as Moscow poured funds and subsidies into eastern Europe in an effort to buttress communist rule in the region. The Soviet 'empire' in eastern Europe was, as many writers have pointed out, very strange indeed – an empire in which the metropolitan power was economically exploited by the 'colonies'.

THE BERLIN CRISIS, 1958–61

The next crisis to afflict Khrushchev was one of his own making, if not entirely of his own choosing. In November 1958 Khrushchev demanded that the USSR and the western powers negotiate and conclude a peace treaty with Germany (there was a surrender agreement dating from 1945 but no final peace settlement). Khrushchev also demanded that the treaty include an agreement to transform West Berlin into an international, demilitarised city. If this was not done within six months, the Soviets threatened to sign a separate accord with the GDR and to turn over control of access to West Berlin to the East German authorities. Khrushchev's demands provoked the second Berlin crisis – the threat of a new blockade which could endanger western control of West Berlin. It was a crisis finally resolved only with the building of the Berlin Wall in August 1961 – a barrier which became a potent symbol of the cold war and the division of Europe.

Khrushchev's immediate purpose was to bolster the East German communist regime, ideally by dislodging the western powers from Berlin or, at a minimum, by involving the GDR in control over the city as a whole – a city which, after all, was located deep inside East German territory. Khrushchev may also have entertained broader objectives: forcing the west to negotiate over the future of Germany; disrupting NATO's planned nuclearisation of West Germany; generally strengthening the Soviet position in central and eastern Europe following the events of 1956. However, as James L. Richardson pointed out in the mid-1960s, during the crisis the Soviets pursued no such broader goals in any consistent manner. His conclusion was that the Berlin crisis showed that 'Soviet objectives tend to be fluid, extravagant ambitions being counterbalanced by reluctance to run risks, success breeding great expectations, failure a readiness to make the best of the status quo' (Richardson, 1966 p. 301).

Richardson's argument has been augmented by more recent research which has shown that an important player in the crisis was Walter Ulbricht, the East German communist leader. Ulbricht pressurised Khrushchev into taking action over West Berlin and at crucial moments during the crisis undertook or threatened unilateral, provocative action which forced Khrushchev's hand. Ulbricht, it seems, played a particularly important role in the decisions leading to the building of the Berlin Wall. The Wall was built to seal the GDR's borders and prevent the 'escape' to the west of hundreds of thousands of East Germans – a migration which was undermining both the economy and the political prestige of the communist state. It was also as, Hope Harrison argues (Harrison article, 1995), a way of sealing in Ulbricht and the East German communist party, of preventing actions by them which might provoke conflict with the western powers.

Khrushchev's November 1958 ultimatum to the western powers was followed by a series of (deadlocked) Soviet–western negotiations on the German question and on the future status of West Berlin. In these negotiations the Soviets proposed peace treaties with the GDR and FRG, a confederation between the two Germanies, the withdrawal of both from NATO and the Warsaw Pact, and the internationalisation and demilitarisation of West Berlin. The western counter-proposal was a united Germany and all-German elections (which the communists had no hope of winning), together with a degree of German disarmament.

For a period the crisis rumbled on at a fairly low level of intensity. In June 1961, however, events took a new turn when Khrushchev abruptly reinstated the six-month deadline on the signature of a peace treaty (it had been dropped while negotiations were in progress). This came in the immediate wake of a summit between Khrushchev and President Kennedy in Vienna at which it became obvious that a negotiated solution of the Berlin problem was not in sight. In response to Khrushchev's ultimatum, Kennedy announced that the US would, if necessary, fight for Berlin. Both sides took steps to strengthen their military posture. Neither side had in mind an actual military conflict, but a war of nerves over Berlin had certainly begun.

As the crisis intensified more and more refugees crossed from East to

West Germany, many via West Berlin. In the 1950s between 100,000 and 200,000 East Germans had migrated west annually. In the summer of 1961 that rate more than doubled. It was this developing crisis – which was economically debilitating and politically demoralising for the East German regime – that led to the building of the Wall. The GDR's communist leaders had long been pressing for decisive action to seal their borders. Now Ulbricht told Khrushchev that if this did not happen the communist regime would fall. On 5 August, a meeting of the members of the Warsaw Pact issued a statement urging the GDR to 'establish on the frontiers of West Berlin a procedure that would reliably close the road to subversion against the countries of the socialist community'. On 13 August construction of this 'procedure' began. The Wall stood for 28 years, until another refugee crisis caused it to come tumbling down.

In the end, for Moscow the only thing that really mattered in the Berlin crisis was safeguarding the future of East Germany. As Soviet Politburo member Anastas Mikoyan put it at the height of the crisis: 'if socialism does not triumph in the GDR, if communism does not prove itself superior and vital here, then we have not won' (Harrison article, 1995). The Berlin Wall was hardly a great advertisement for socialism, but it kept alive the East German communist regime and with it Khrushchev's belief that in the long term the economic and political competition with the west could be won.

THE SINO-SOVIET SPLIT

Berlin was not the only international crisis of 1958. On the other side of the world another threatening east–west conflict exploded into the open. In August 1958 the People's Republic of China (PRC – communist-controlled mainland China) began shelling the Quemoy and Matsu islands in the straits of Taiwan. These islands were occupied by Chiang Kai-shek's Nationalist forces, which had been ensconced in Taiwan since their defeat by the communists in the Chinese civil war of 1945–9. It seemed that the PRC was about to carry out its longstanding threat to invade Taiwan and unify all Chinese territory under communist control. In response the United States reinforced its naval and air units in the straits and reaffirmed its commitment to defend Taiwan from external attack.

This was not the first 'Quemoy crisis'. In 1954 there had been a similar military incident. On both occasions the USSR made clear its support for China and announced it would fulfil its defence obligations under the 1950 Sino-Soviet Treaty of Friendship, Alliance and

Mutual Assistance. On 7 September 1958 Khrushchev warned Eisenhower that an American attack on China would be considered an attack on the Soviet Union itself. But behind this impressive show of solidarity there were concerns in Moscow about China's handling of the crisis.

Traditionally, the historical literature has depicted Soviet worries about the crisis as focusing on the provocative nature of the Chinese action in shelling Quemoy and Matsu islands. More recent documentation indicates, however, that what Moscow really objected to was the failure of the Chinese communists to consult them about the timing and purpose of the action. The Soviets were also disappointed when the Chinese quickly backed away from the confrontation in the face of strong American support for Chiang Kai-shek (the crisis petered out in October 1958). Moscow was also worried about statements made to the Soviet Foreign Minister, Andrei Gromyko, in Beijing on 7 September 1958. The PRC Prime Minister and Foreign Minister, Zhou Enlai, told Gromyko that the USSR should become involved in a Chinese–American war only if the US used *strategic* nuclear weapons against China, i.e. that the Soviet Union should not launch a nuclear strike against the United States if the Americans used only *tactical* or battlefield nuclear weapons. This stance struck Moscow as dangerous from a number of points of view.

First, it undermined the deterrent effect of the threat of massive nuclear retaliation in the event of a US attack on China. The possibility of going to war with China and being able to use tactical nuclear weapons without fear of strategic nuclear retaliation by the USSR could encourage the Americans to initiate such a conflict. Second, it undermined the absolute unity of the communist bloc on matters of common defence. As a letter from the Soviet communist party to the Chinese communist party in September 1958 put it: 'the main thing now consists of the fact that . . . we are firm and united in our understanding of the tasks, which flow from Marxist-Leninist teaching, to defend the camp of socialism, that the unity of all brother Communist parties is unshakeable, that we will visit a joint, decisive rebuff to the aggressor in the event of an attack on any socialist state.' Third, decoupling Soviet and Chinese involvement in the event of war with the United States was also undesirable because it gave Beijing more scope for independent foreign policy action. If the USSR was not bound under all circumstances to enter a Chinese–American war then China was not bound under all circumstances to accept a Soviet veto of action that might precipitate such a war. This was the nub of the developing tension in the Sino-Soviet alliance: how much autonomy was

China to have in its relationship with its big, communist brother, the USSR?

The Quemoy crisis was far from being the first occasion for friction in the Sino-Soviet relationship. During the long years of their struggle for power in the 1920s and 1930s the Chinese communist leadership had often clashed with Stalin and Moscow over matters of revolutionary strategy and tactics. At the time of the Korean War there had been significant differences over Chinese support for North Korea and about the extent of Soviet military aid to communist forces. To an extent, Beijing had felt badgered by the Soviets into engaging a war in which they shouldered the main burden of defence of the communist bloc. Neither was Chinese communist leader Mao Zedong very happy about Khrushchev's denunciation of Stalin (which he thought was an opportunist move which did the Soviet dictator an injustice) and he did not agree with the Soviet leader's new conception of peaceful coexistence – which he thought underplayed the role of war and violence in the world wide struggle for socialism. There were also differences between the Soviet and Chinese comrades over the building of socialism in China. The Soviets disapproved of Mao's Great Leap Forward, an economic programme introduced in January 1958. This aimed to industrialise China by developing small-scale manufacturing in peasant communes. Such deviations from the Soviet model of socialist economic development (large-scale, concentrated and centrally directed urban-industrial production) were never welcomed by Moscow. They legitimised the possibility of alternatives to the Soviet model of socialism.

The accumulation of such tensions and differences did not augur well for the future of the Sino-Soviet alliance in the late 1950s. But the subsequent schism, split and enmity was precipitated by more than these problems. It was a specific series of events in the summer and autumn of 1959 which precipitated the conflict. Of particular importance was the Sino-Indian border conflict of July–October 1959. A longstanding dispute about the line of the frontier between India and Chinese-occupied Tibet in the Himalayas came to a head in 1959 following a large-scale but unsuccessful uprising against Chinese rule in Tibet, which resulted in the flight to India of the Tibetan leader, the Dalai Lama. Although there were only very minor clashes between Chinese and Indian forces along the border, the dispute threatened a Sino-Indian border war (one actually broke out in 1962). Moscow's problem was that it was trying to cultivate an alliance with India, one of the leading countries in the non-aligned movement. Hence in September 1959 the Soviet news agency, TASS, issued a statement calling for a peaceful resolution of the dispute, a call which was interpreted by the Chinese as a declaration of neutrality. In Beijing they were outraged by this breach in communist solidarity:

> the Tass statement showed to the whole world the different positions of China and the Soviet Union in regard to the incident on the Indian–Chinese border, which causes a virtual glee and jubilation among the Indian bourgeoisie and the American and the English imperialists who are in every way driving a wedge between China and the Soviet Union.

So argued the central committee of the Chinese communist party in a letter to the Soviet communist party central committee in September 1959.

The summer of 1959 also witnessed the beginning of Soviet back-tracking on previous commitments to aid China's nuclear weapons development programme. A series of Sino-Soviet agreements to this effect had been signed in the mid-1950s. But when it came to the crunch of handing over to the Chinese prototypes and plans of atomic bombs, Moscow began to have second thoughts. Was it wise, the Soviets must have thought, to provide such weapons to a government headed by a man who didn't seem to fear a third world war, who thought US imperialism was a 'paper tiger' (albeit one with nuclear teeth, as Khrushchev famously quipped)?

These developments formed the background to Khrushchev's visit to Beijing in October 1959 to join in the celebrations of the tenth anniversary of the establishment of the PRC. In Beijing, sharp disagreements arose over the fate of Taiwan (Moscow now favoured a peaceful resolution of that dispute), over the Sino-Indian dispute, and over peaceful coexistence and the nuclear threat. Perhaps most important from the Soviet point of view was the breakdown in personal and comradely relations that occurred. An attitude of fraternal, if sometimes fragile, solidarity between Chinese and Soviet communists was replaced by an atmosphere of mistrust and suspicion. On his return to Moscow Khrushchev began to withdraw Soviet scientific and technical experts from China. In July 1960 Moscow informed Beijing that such Soviet specialists in China (there were many thousands of them) were to be recalled. One of the main reasons given for this action was that Chinese officials had attempted to indoctrinate Soviet personnel on certain ideological issues. This was a reference to the growing ideological split between the USSR and China which came into public view in spring 1960 with the publication of an article in the Chinese communist newspaper *Red Flag* on 'Long Live Leninism' – a thinly disguised critique of Khrushchev's peaceful coexistence policy.

The public face of this early phase of the Sino-Soviet split was not foreign policy differences or inter-state conflicts but ideological disputes about communist principles and strategy, particularly in relation to the anti-imperialist struggle in the third world. As Mark Kramer has argued, these 'ideological aspects of the conflict must be taken seriously on their own merits, rather than being seen as a mere smokescreen for geopolitical or other concerns' (Kramer article, 1995–6 p. 171).

The Sino-Soviet ideological polemics were mainly conducted in the communist press, but also found an airing at communist conferences and other gatherings. Often the Soviet and Chinese attacks on each other's position were veiled and indirect. The Soviets, for example, directed a lot of fire at the Albanian communist party, which had sided with China in the dispute, while the Chinese targeted Yugoslavia and the west European communist parties. Leaders and members of other communist parties joined in the argument. The PRC and its supporters in the communist movement accused the Soviet Union of 'opportunism' and 'revisionism'. The Soviets and their allies (by far the great majority of communists) countered with charges of 'ultra-leftism' and 'adventurism'.

At the heart of the ideological dispute was the question about what role violence and war played in the revolutionary transition to socialism. The Chinese rejected the concept of a peaceful road to socialism and the idea that the danger of war had lessened in the nuclear age. The reactionary, nasty nature of capitalism and imperialism ensured, they argued, that civil wars, colonial wars, national liberation wars, even inter-capitalist wars were natural and inevitable. A general, nuclear war between socialism and capitalism was not inevitable, but even if one did occur, that would not necessarily mean the end of civilisation and socialist progress; out of the ashes of war had arisen both revolutionary Russia and communist China. Moreover, the Chinese argued, fear of catastrophic war did not make one less likely; it encouraged the enemy and resulted in paralysis in the face of imperialist threats. For their part, the Russians stressed the destructive danger of nuclear war, argued that violent, armed struggle was not the only way to achieve socialism and accused the Chinese of bravado and brinkmanship.

The Sino-Soviet ideological conflict did not immediately result in a political and diplomatic split between the two countries. In foreign policy terms the Sino-Soviet alliance was outwardly maintained. China supported the USSR in both the Berlin and Cuban crises (although with no great enthusiasm), while Moscow displayed restraint and understanding to Beijing when the Sino-Indian frontier dispute flared into a border war in September–November 1962. In 1962–3 there were several attempts (mainly on Soviet initiative) to end the public polemics and normalise relations. But these efforts were stymied by an important development in east–west relations. In August 1963 Britain, the Soviet Union and the United States signed a 'Treaty Banning Nuclear Weapons Tests in the Atmosphere, in Outer Space and Under Water'. About the same time, there was much talk of a nuclear non-proliferation treaty (one was actually signed in 1968). These developments were seen in Beijing as further Soviet efforts to prevent China from acquiring nuclear weapons (which it did in October 1964 when it tested its first A-bomb).

Conflict about the non-proliferation talks and the test ban treaty led to the resumption and intensification of the ideological polemics. Each side began to accuse the other of national-chauvinism, of playing power politics and of undermining the anti-capitalist and anti-imperialist struggle. The Chinese even accused the Russians of restoring capitalism in the USSR! The ideological dispute escalated to a formal split in the world communist movement as a number of parties and factions within parties backed the 'Maoist' line. In March 1966 the Soviet and Chinese communist parties severed their fraternal party ties. The communist bloc had definitively split (although only Albania definitely aligned itself with China). Chinese foreign policy became increasingly defined by its anti-Sovietism and by a campaign against so-called Soviet 'social imperialism'. In Moscow the Soviet leadership decided to build up their military forces on the frontier with China. Soviet nuclear missiles were relocated eastwards and retargeted on China. There was even talk in Moscow of the desirability of a joint Soviet–American pre-emptive nuclear strike against China. This was wild talk but in March 1969 there were extensive Russian–Chinese military clashes along the Sino-Soviet border. The decade-long transition of the two communist giants from alliance to enmity was complete.

THE CUBAN MISSILE CRISIS

For all the Russian accusations of Mao Tse Tung's adventurism and brinkmanship, it was Khrushchev's actions – and Kennedy's reaction to them – which brought the world closest to the brink of nuclear war. In May 1962 Khrushchev and the Soviet political-military leadership agreed a plan to secretly deploy a substantial number of nuclear missiles in Cuba. Shipment of the missiles and their deployment in Cuba – the Soviets called it 'Operation Anadyr' – began a few weeks later. By October 1962 there were over 150 strategic and tactical nuclear weapons sited in Cuba, together with 40,000 Soviet troops and an array of conventional weapons including fighter and bomber aircraft. But American reconnaissance flights discovered Operation Anadyr while it was still in progress. On 22 October President Kennedy announced the discovery of the missiles, demanded their removal and imposed a naval blockade of Cuba to stop further missile shipments. Following a tense exchange of messages, on 27–8 October Kennedy and Khrushchev agreed a deal: the Soviet missiles would be withdrawn in exchange for an American promise not to invade Cuba. There was also a secret deal that US Jupiter missiles in Turkey would be removed. The crisis was over.

McGeorge Bundy, Kennedy's National Security Advisor, subsequently estimated that the risk of nuclear war during the crisis may have been as low as 100-1 – short odds indeed on the end of civilisation as we know it. Why did Khrushchev, acutely aware as he was of the dangers posed by the existence of such weapons of mass destruction, take such a risk? His given reason at the time, which he restated in his memoirs, was that the main purpose of the missile deployment was to deter an American invasion of Cuba. The background here was the establishment of a socialist regime in Cuba following the seizure of power by Fidel Castro's left-wing guerrilla army in January 1959. Castro was not a communist but he subsequently became one and came into conflict with the US when he nationalised American businesses in Cuba. US–Cuban relations deteriorated sharply and broke down completely when, in April 1961, the Americans sponsored an attempted invasion by Cuban émigrés at the Bay of Pigs. Meanwhile, Castro had turned to Moscow for economic aid and military support. The Soviets, committed to supporting socialist-leaning regimes such as Cuba and keen to secure a foothold in the Americans' Caribbean backyard, were more than happy to oblige.

Since 1962 a mountain of material has been published on the Cuban missile crisis, including many memoirs and archive documents from the Soviet side of the story. But there is still no real reason to doubt the veracity of Khrushchev's own account: that Cuba was seen to be under threat of an American invasion and that the missiles were placed there to deter such an attack and to maintain Fidel Castro in power. Nor is there any reason to question the sincerity of Khrushchev's ideological and personal motives; this really was a genuine act of Soviet socialist solidarity. There is even evidence that at one point Khrushchev seriously contemplated the prospect of going nuclear in order to defend Cuba from an American invasion (Fursenko and Naftali article, 1998).

Khrushchev's commitment to defend socialist Cuba come what may, does not rule out additional motives and calculations. In his memoirs

Khrushchev mentions one himself: restoring the strategic nuclear balance with the United States – this was a time when the Americans were way ahead of the Russians in numbers of bombs, planes, missiles and warheads. It has also been suggested that Khrushchev may have felt that a strong stand in support of Cuba was a necessary riposte to Chinese and to domestic critics of his foreign policy (particularly of its failure in the Berlin crisis). But perhaps the overriding ulterior motive was that indicated by two Russian historians, Vladislav Zubok and Constantine Pleshakov: Khrushchev's sense of rivalry and competition with the United States. In the context of the grand cold war contest there could be no question of allowing socialist Cuba to go under, even if that meant a risky nuclear gamble. Equally, one should not underestimate the importance of the calculative element in Khrushchev's reasoning and decision-making. Presumably, he thought that the action would work and that he could get away with it (i.e. the unveiling of a fully deployed missile force in Cuba would deter the Americans and would *de facto* be accepted by them). Here Khrushchev miscalculated the political and psychological impact of the missiles on Washington. He was used to the idea of living with US nuclear airbases and missile units on his doorstep in Europe and Turkey, but the Americans were not accustomed to the idea of Soviet missiles in their backyard.

When the crisis was over Khrushchev suggested to Kennedy the negotiation of a grand diplomatic bargain which would resolve a number of Soviet–American disputes and reduce international tension. He proposed a summit, even a non-aggression pact between the Soviet Union and the United States. His aim was to pick up the thread of détente from the mid-1950s, which had come perilously close to breaking altogether during the crisis years of 1958–62. There was no grand bargain, but there was important progress in the fields of arms control (the test ban treaty and non-proliferation talks) and crisis management (the installation of the Kremlin–White House telephone 'hotline'). Above all there was the recognition by both sides that the cold war, nuclear weapons and competitive coexistence required mutual restraint and regulation. Here was the beginning of the road leading to the Soviet–American détente of the 1970s.

NUCLEAR POLITICS

Cuba was a nuclear crisis in every sense. The crisis was caused by the Soviet decision to deploy nuclear missiles in Cuba. The political aim of the deployment was to use the danger and threat of nuclear war to deter an American invasion of Cuba. The United States responded in the way it did because of the perceived impact of the deployment on the Soviet–American nuclear balance of power. There was no danger of deliberate escalation of the crisis into a nuclear war (although it did not seem like that at the time), but on both sides there were very real dangers of inadvertent, unauthorised or accidental use of nuclear weaponry. It was precisely for this reason that the Cuban missile crisis was the first and last nuclear crisis of the cold war. The nuclear brink was far too dangerous a place to perch.

Cuba was not Khrushchev's first attempt to use nuclear war power for political ends. Before 1962 there had been a whole series of Soviet nuclear sabre rattling exercises. At the height of the Suez crisis in 1956 the Soviets made threatening (but essentially rhetorical) noises about the use of nuclear rockets against the British and French in defence of their Egyptian ally. Soviet support for the PRC in the 1954 and 1958 Quemoy crises amounted to an implicit threat of nuclear retaliation should the Americans launch an attack on China. The same applied to the Berlin crisis, in which Khrushchev attempted to utilise the danger of a nuclear confrontation as a bargaining chip in negotiations on the fate of Germany. Another tactic was demonstrations of Soviet nuclear capability to project the presence and power of the USSR in world politics. Soviet nuclear missiles were regularly paraded in Red Square. In October 1961, at the height of the Berlin crisis and as the twenty-second congress of the communist party met in Moscow, the Soviets exploded a 50 megaton H-bomb – the largest ever nuclear test.

There was, however, a large element of bluff in Soviet nuclear diplomacy. Throughout the Khrushchev era the USSR remained far behind the US in terms of bombs, warheads and delivery systems. It is true that the Soviets had successfully tested the first Intercontinental Ballistic Missile (ICBM) in August 1957; indeed, shortly after they had used the same model of rocket to launch the world's first satellite (Sputnik). But only a handful of ICBMs were deployed by the Soviets before the mid-1960s. They did deploy several hundred short and medium range missiles (i.e. incapable of reaching the US, unless based in Cuba) but the Americans had many more planes and rockets at their disposal.

Khrushchev, it seems, was happy to bluff and bluster, partly because that was the way he operated and partly out of necessity. In addition, Khrushchev's idea of nuclear politics was informed by the then prevailing conceptions of the 'balance of terror' and 'massive retaliation'. Provided the Soviet Union was able to inflict mass devastation on the enemy, that was enough to deter a nuclear attack on the USSR and enough of a threat to deploy for political purposes. The threat of mutual annihilation was also sufficient to minimise the danger of the outbreak of a nuclear war (although the Cuba crisis had placed a question mark over that assumption). After Cuba and after Khrushchev, the Soviet concept of deterrence changed. The credibility of the nuclear deterrent came to be seen as of central importance – and credibility was defined by the achievement and maintenance of strategic nuclear parity with the United States. With this shift there came a new nuclear politics. Nuclear capability was now a matter of security and prestige, not defence and diplomacy. Certainly there was no question of projecting nuclear power for political purposes. That was far too perilous in conditions of parity. Nor was it desirable at all, given the immense dangers and meagre results achieved by Khrushchev's atomic diplomacy.

At the heart of the policy shift was a change in the concept of 'parity', which now became defined as equality in numbers and quality of weapons (as opposed to Khrushchev's concept which was in terms of retaliatory destructive power) How and why this shift in nuclear policy came about is not yet entirely clear. It may be that Soviet nuclear inferiority in terms of missiles was seen as inhibiting in the confrontation with the Americans over Cuba. Probably, the influence of Soviet military strategists was important to the change in deterrence doctrine. Perhaps the growth in Soviet technical and manufacturing capabilities played a role. It is very likely, too, that the Soviets were responding to the expansion and diversification of the US and NATO nuclear arsenals. In any event the mid to late 1960s was a period of a massive Soviet nuclear buildup, particularly of ICBMs. By the end of the decade the USSR had over 1000 ICBMs, as well as hundreds of short and medium range nuclear missiles. The missile gap with the United States had been closed, strategic nuclear parity achieved. It was an achievement that the post-Khrushchev leadership was determined to maintain. At the same time, Moscow continued, indeed intensified its search for a less confrontational, more co-operative and positive relationship with the United States. Massive nuclear arsenals and strategic nuclear parity were to be balanced by an end to the cold war and the launch of a new era of détente.

4 The rise and fall of détente, 1964–85

The struggle to consolidate the principles
of peaceful coexistence, to assure lasting peace,
and to reduce and in the long term to eliminate
the danger of world war remains the main element
of our policy towards the capitalist states.
Considerable progress has been achieved in the
past five years. The passage from the cold war . . .
to détente was primarily connected with changes in
the correlation of world forces. . . . Though world
peace is by no means guaranteed yet, we have
every reason to declare that the improvement of
the international climate is convincing evidence
that lasting peace is not merely a good intention
but an entirely realistic objective.

Our Party gives support and will continue to support
peoples fighting for their liberation. . . . Some bourgeois
figures express surprise and raise a storm over the
solidarity of Soviet communists, the Soviet people,
with the struggle of other peoples and progress. That
is either naive or, more likely, deliberate confusion.
It is crystal clear that détente and peaceful
coexistence concern interstate relations. . . . Détente does
not and cannot in the slightest abolish or change the
laws of the class struggle.

(L.I. Brezhnev, report to the twenty-fifth congress of the
CPSU, February–March 1976)

OVERVIEW

Khrushchev was ousted from power in October 1964 when a meeting of
the party central committee removed him from office. The new First

Secretary of the communist party was Leonid Brezhnev (in 1966 his title was changed to General Secretary), while Alexei Kosygin became head of the government. During the 1960s it was common to refer to the Brezhnev-Kosygin leadership of the Soviet Union. By the 1970s, however, Brezhnev was firmly established as *primus inter pares* in the Soviet leadership.

Khrushchev's dismissal was a consequence of domestic differences and power struggles rather than foreign policy setbacks, but his failure to achieve Soviet aims in the Berlin and Cuban crises did contribute to his downfall. Neither did Khrushchev's overbearing, personalised conduct of foreign policy endear him to others in the Soviet leadership. By contrast, under Brezhnev, Soviet foreign policy was less idiosyncratic and individual and decision-making more regularised and institutionalised than it had been under Khrushchev. Brezhnev's personal style was that of a conciliator and a consensus seeker. His rule was the most collective of any Soviet leader, including in the field of foreign policy.

After his death in 1982 Brezhnev's period in office came to be depicted (not least in the Soviet Union itself) as years of political, economic and social stagnation. Certainly, the Khrushchevite programme of destalinisation and partial liberalisation ground to a halt in the 1960s. It is also true that consolidation and incremental advance rather than radical reform and rapid forward movement were the hallmarks of Brezhnev's domestic policy. In the foreign policy sphere, however, the Brezhnev leadership showed considerable initiative and dynamism. As Jonathan Steele has argued, the USSR of the Khrushchev era remained a continental rather than a global power, whereas 'under Leonid Brezhnev the Soviet Union became a world power' – a military superpower engaged in a global competition with the United States for power and influence (Steele, 1985 p. ix).

While in many ways different, the Brezhnev era in Soviet foreign policy was no less dramatic and crisis-ridden than the Khrushchev period. It was an era of Soviet involvement in a series of wars and military actions: Vietnam, Czechoslovakia, the Sino-Soviet border, the Middle East, Angola, the Horn of Africa, Afghanistan. There were other crises as well; most notably, the Polish crisis of 1980–1 provoked by Solidarity's challenge to communist control and the tension in Europe following Warsaw Pact and NATO decisions to deploy a new generation of nuclear missiles (respectively, Soviet SS20s and American Cruise and Pershing missiles).

But while the cold war heated up from time to time, there was never any question of east–west rivalry getting out of hand, of there being a repeat of dangerous confrontations akin to the Berlin and Cuban crises. This was because, above all else, the Brezhnev period was an era of détente.

From the late 1960s through to the mid-1970s there was a significant reduction in cold war tensions, the settlement of a number of disputes arising out of the postwar settlement in Europe, joint Soviet–American efforts to control the arms race, and the development of east–west economic, diplomatic and political interchange and co-operation. These developments were collectively characterised as an east–west 'détente'; indeed, at the time they were hailed by many as signifying the end of the cold war. The most potent symbol of détente was a series of American–Soviet summits at which Brezhnev and a succession of US presidents jointly proclaimed their mutual commitment to co-operation not confrontation.

From the Soviet point of view détente was, ideologically speaking, a specific form of peaceful coexistence involving peaceful collaboration with capitalism as well as peaceful competition. It did not mean an end to political change and development. Nor did détente signify the abandonment of the Soviet Union's socialist aspirations. On the contrary, détente was seen as both an outcome of the historic, global process leading towards socialism and as providing a favourable context for further socialist progress. Hence, Moscow reserved the right to pursue its ideological and political ambitions while at the same time maintaining positive, peaceful relations with the capitalist states. In this respect there was an elemental continuity between the Khrushchev and Brezhnev eras. Under Brezhnev, however, the Soviets had both greater capabilities and were presented with more opportunities to aid 'progressive forces' in different parts of the globe. More resources were available for such Soviet interventionism and during the 1960s and 1970s the USSR's logistical capabilities, militarily and otherwise, increased dramatically. Ultimately, the USSR's pursuit of a global policy proved to be a serious strain on the Soviet economy, but during Brezhnev's time expanding Moscow's world-wide influence was seen as politically worth its financial cost and ideologically as a natural part of the flow of history in the direction of communism.

From the very beginning, détente had its conservative critics in the west who characterised it as a mask behind which the Soviets hid their ambitions for expansion and subversion. By the late 1970s anti-détente elements were in the ascendency in many western countries, most importantly in the United States. One of the most prominent critics of détente was Ronald Reagan, who defeated Jimmy Carter in the 1980 US presidential election. In January 1981 he stated that so far détente's been a one-way street which the Soviet Union has used to pursue its own aims. I know of no leader of the Soviet Union . . . that has not more than once repeated in the various Communist congresses they hold, their determination that their goal must be the promotion of world revolution and a one-world Socialist or Communist state.

(Garthoff, 1994, pp. 8–9)

He went on to accuse Soviet leaders of being willing to crime, lie, and cheat in order to achieve their aims. Later, in 1983, Reagan famously referred to the USSR as an 'evil empire'.

The rise of anti-détente forces in the west was a worrying development for Moscow, but even after Reagan's election Soviet faith remained strong that détente was an irreversible development in world politics that was rooted in a fundamental shift in the balance of forces in the Soviet Union's favour. It was a faith that blinkered Moscow's perception of the contribution made by its own actions to the gradual erosion of détente from the mid-1970s onwards, although some in the Soviet leadership, for example Mikhail Gorbachev, did have doubts about Soviet policy, particularly in the third world.

Détente failed because it was abandoned as a policy by the west, not least by Reagan's America. The process of western disengagement from détente was gradual, but was connected to a series of Soviet miscalculations and misadventures. In 1976 the Soviets began the deployment of a new generation of Intermediate Range Ballistic Missiles (the RSD-10 or SS20 as it was called in the west) in eastern Europe and the western USSR. This provoked a NATO counter-response (the deployment of Pershing and Cruise missiles) and undermined efforts to control the nuclear arms race in Europe. The mid-1970s also saw a massive programme of Soviet military assistance to a series of embattled leftist regimes in Africa and the Middle East. In the cases of Angola and Ethiopia this involved the use of Cuban combat troops as well as many thousands of Soviet military specialists and advisers. Western opponents of détente depicted these projections of Soviet military power as part of a programme of global communist expansionism. At the end of 1979, the USSR embarked on a major military operation in Afghanistan designed to prop up an ailing leftist regime under threat from Islamic guerrillas. In protest, the US and a number of other countries boycotted the 1980 Olympic Games in Moscow. (In 1984 the Soviet Union and its allies retaliated with a boycott of the Los Angeles Olympics). While the Soviets did not invade Poland in order to crush Solidarity, the hand of Moscow was very much behind the organisation's banning and the imprisonment of its leaders following the imposition of martial law by the communist authorities in December 1981.

From Moscow's point of view all these actions were legitimate reactions to situations which required action to protect Soviet security interests or fell within the bounds of competitive coexistence. It is important to remember, too, that the Soviets were far from the only players in the situations in which they became embroiled. The Americans practised their own brand of global interventionism and the projection of military power and political influence. In 1973 a CIA programme of covert action was instrumental in the military coup which overthrew the regime of Salvador Allende, the Marxist President of Chile. A different example is the American detachment of Egypt from its alliance with the USSR following the Yom Kippur War of 1973. The Soviets had since the 1950s been rendering the Egyptians considerable economic and military aid and had supported them politically and materially at the time of the Suez Crisis in 1956 as well as in the Arab–Israeli wars of 1967 and 1973. The loss of the Egyptian connection was a devastating blow to the Soviet position in the Middle East. But Moscow made no public complaint about it, at least not in connection with détente and peaceful coexistence (privately, however, the Soviets were furious and anxious to compensate for the loss of Egypt by seeking allies elsewhere in the Middle East). Competitive coexistence cut both ways. It was a competition in which Moscow accepted its losses as well as its gains.

But as with the origins of the cold war, what to Moscow were reactive, defensive or limited moves were perceived by many in the west as aggressive and threatening. The result was the outbreak in the early 1980s of what some commentators called a new, or second, cold war in which east–west rivalry, tension and suspicion were once more to the fore. It was not an outcome welcomed by Moscow, which remained deeply committed to détente and continued to value the significant political, economic, military and ideological benefits it had, for a time, brought to the Soviet state.

ORIGINS OF DÉTENTE

Moscow's pursuit of détente in the 1960s and 1970s was a continuation of the peaceful coexistence line of Soviet foreign policy. The Soviet desire for détente was neither new nor surprising. Indeed, in a sense détente had been the defining goal of Soviet foreign policy throughout the cold war – a détente on the Soviets' own terms, of course. But there were also specific reasons and incentives for the Soviets to embrace détente in the 1970s. These are well summarised by R. Craig Nation (1992 pp. 256–8):

1 *To stabilise the arms race once approximate strategic parity with the United States was achieved.* (There were limits to the Soviet capacity to compete with the US in an ever-more costly and technologically driven nuclear arms race. Soviet fear of the danger of nuclear war should also never be underestimated as a motive for participation in arms control negotiations and the creation of east–west crisis management procedures.)

2 *To win international acceptance of the postwar security order in Europe.* (The aim here was to stabilise and solidify the cold war division of Europe on the basis of existing territorial and bloc demarcation lines and to establish pan-European collective security arrangements.)

3 *To create a more propitious climate for east–west trade and technology transfer.* (By the 1960s the Soviet and East European economies had entered the stage of qualitative rather than quantitative economic development, which entailed more emphasis on the satisfaction of consumer demands and on technological and industrial innovation. The USSR needed the external economic input of the west.)

4 *To neutralise the threat of US–Chinese collusion by giving the West a greater stake in positive relations with USSR.* (Following the Sino-Soviet split a recurrent Moscow nightmare was a Sino-American alliance directed against the USSR. Soviet efforts to nullify American playing of the 'China Card' was one of the great themes of détente diplomacy and Soviet–American relations in the 1970s.)

Détente was, of course, an international phenomenon and Soviet motives were only one of the factors at play in its creation. Crucially, the Americans had their own reasons for seeking détente. Of decisive importance was the foreign policy strategy of Richard Nixon, elected US President in 1968, and his National Security Advisor, Henry Kissinger. They devised a project for managing Soviet power: of creating a new international order with built-in incentives for restrained Soviet behaviour. In their conception, the price of détente was the maintenance of the international status quo and a curtailment of Soviet expansionary and revolutionary ambitions. (Unfortunately, Moscow did not see détente in these terms. The Soviet aim was to manage American power in a way that facilitated the possibility of peaceful political change in a socialist direction.) Nixon and Kissinger also counted on Soviet help in securing an acceptable settlement of the

Vietnam conflict and calculated that threatening co-operation with China was a trump card that they would be able to play effectively in negotiations with Moscow. (The Soviets made a similar calculation regarding the Americans' troubles in Vietnam.)

Another major player in the creation of détente was western Europe. Detente as a concept is most often associated with the significant improvement in Soviet–American relations which occurred in the 1970s. But there were parallel developments in Europe. Indeed, the inception of the European détente predated the Soviet–American détente and in many ways provided the foundation for the latter.

Détente is, of course, a French word deriving from the verb détendre meaning, variously, to unbend, to slacken, to loosen, to unstring, to relax, to become milder, easier. It is a traditional word in the vocabulary of diplomacy used to describe a relaxation of tensions between states. In the modern era its use was popularised as a description of the policy of President Charles de Gaulle in the mid-1960s whose aim was to overcome the cold war divisions in Europe (and in that context, to assert French independence from the US and French leadership in Europe). De Gaulle's efforts in this respect included a number of conciliatory gestures towards the Soviet Union and the eastern bloc. De Gaulle did not achieve much of political and diplomatic substance but he did contribute to a better, more hopeful atmosphere which encouraged the Soviets to persist with their longstanding design of an all-European collective security system.

The next major set of developments in the progress to a European détente arose out of Willy Brandt's policy of *Ostpolitik* (eastern policy). This was the policy pursued by Brandt after he became Chancellor of West Germany in 1969. It basically consisted of a policy of reconciliation and the development of relations and ties with the USSR, the GDR and other eastern bloc states. *Ostpolitik*'s concrete results included a Soviet–West German renunciation of force treaty (i.e. a non-aggression pact) in August 1970; the FRG's recognition of Poland's western border (which incorporated much prewar German territory) in December 1970; the conclusion in September 1971 of a final settlement of the Berlin question (basically, the continuation of four-power control and the east–west division of the former German capital); and, in December 1972, an FRG–GDR agreement on mutual recognition, which paved the way for the admission of both states as members of the United Nations. None of this would have been possible in the absence of a positive Soviet response to Brandt's various initiatives.

On the broader front of European détente the most important development was the inauguration in Helsinki in July 1973 of the first round of talks of the Conference on Security and Co-operation in Europe (CSCE). This pan-European conference involved representatives of all European states (except Albania) plus Canada, the US and the Vatican. The conference concluded with the signature in August 1975 of a wide-ranging agreement (the Helsinki Accord) on the peaceful and co-operative principles which should govern relations between European states; on east–west confidence building measures in the field of security and disarmament; on economic, scientific and environmental cooperation; and on respect for human rights and the encouragement of people-to-people contacts in Europe. Not everything in the CSCE agreement was to Soviet liking (for example, in relation to the protection of human rights, which Moscow saw as a device for western interference in its internal affairs). But the Warsaw Pact had been campaigning for such a conference since the 1950s and Helsinki was viewed by Moscow as a significant success for Soviet diplomacy and as one of the high points of détente. Particularly pleasing for the Soviets were the CSCE agreements' underwriting of the territorial and political status quo in Europe – a final rubberstamping of the *de facto* post-Second World War peace settlement which had emerged during the early years of the cold war.

Whatever it might mean to Moscow in other contexts, détente in Europe was about freezing the outcome of the cold war and the maintenance on a stable, predictable and orderly basis of Soviet control of eastern Europe. Moscow's determination that détente should underwrite its position in eastern Europe had, in fact, only very recently been reinforced by events in Czechoslovakia in 1968 which had revealed once again the fragility of Moscow's communist bloc in eastern Europe.

DÉTENTE DEFLECTED: THE INVASION OF CZECHOSLOVAKIA, 1968

In January 1968 the hardline leader of Czechoslovakia, Antonin Novotny, was replaced by Alexander Dubcek as First Secretary of the communist party. As party leader Dubcek initiated a programme of reform in Czechoslovakia. Dubcek's slogan was 'socialism with a human face'; his aim was the development in Czechoslovakia of a socialist system based on the active consent and participation of the people. The realisation of that aim required the democratisation of the Czechoslovak political and economic system and the reform of the communist party to make it a more open, pluralist organisation, which would rule the country on the basis of popular consent. Dubcek's proposed reforms were set out in 'The Action Programme of the

Communist Party of Czechoslovakia' of April 1968. It was this programme which initiated the so-called 'Prague Spring' in Czechoslovakia – the movement towards a reformed communism which would be free and democratic as well as socialist.

The reform communism of Dubcek and his supporters was not to Moscow's liking, not least because it entailed the rejection of the authoritarian Soviet model of socialism (which had hitherto prevailed in Czechoslovakia) in favour of a westernised, democratic model of socialism. It was yet another challenge to Moscow's ideological guardianship of the world communist movement and of the communist bloc. Yugoslavia, China, Albania, Romania (which began to distance itself from Moscow and the Warsaw Pact in the mid-1960s) and now the Czechoslovaks were trying to assert their national and political independence. Moscow believed, too, that the Prague Spring could get out of hand and, like Hungary in 1956, develop into a 'counter-revolutionary situation', which might spill over into other communist systems in eastern Europe. One of the most disturbing developments of the Prague Spring for Moscow was the abolition in June of the censorship regime in Czechoslovakia. This opened the floodgates to a torrent of criticism in the media of the USSR, of Soviet socialism, of the Warsaw Pact and the Stalinist deformation of the Czechoslovak communist movement. The political organisation of this dissent into parties and movements that would challenge communist control of Czechoslovakia seemed, to Moscow, to be only a matter of time.

As soon as the direction of the Dubcek leadership became clear, the Soviets began to campaign for a slowing down, if not a reversal of the reformist course. Among Moscow's pressure points were Warsaw Pact manoeuvres in Czechoslovakia, with the implied threat of military intervention to nip the Prague Spring in the bud. But Moscow's campaigning was mainly political in character: the publication of highly critical press articles, private lobbying of the Czechoslovak leadership, encouragement to hardline opponents of Dubcek within the communist party, and the rallying of east European support for the Soviet position.

The crisis came to a head in summer 1968 and entered its final phase with the 'Warsaw Letter' of 15 July, a letter sent to the Czechoslovak Communist Party (CCP) from the leaders of the communist parties of Bulgaria, the GDR, Hungary, Poland and the USSR, who met in Warsaw on 14–15 July to consider the Czechoslovakian situation. The letter (which was a public statement as well) said:

We are deeply disturbed by the course of events in your country. The offensive of reaction, backed by imperialism, against your party and the foundations of the Czechoslovakia Socialist Republic, threatens . . . to push your country from the road of socialism, and thereby threatens the interests of the entire socialist system. . . .

We cannot reconcile ourselves . . . with the fact of hostile forces pushing your country off the road of socialism and creating a threat of tearing away Czechoslovakia from the socialist community.

This is NO longer only your concern. This is the common concern of all communist and workers' parties and of states united by alliance, co-operation and friendship. . . .

Each of our parties bears responsibility not only before its working class and before its nation, but also before the international working class, the world communist movement, and cannot evade the obligations arising therefrom. That is why we should show solidarity and be united in the defence of the conquest of socialism, of our security and of the international positions of the entire socialist community. This is why we consider that a decisive rebuff to the anti-communist forces and a determined struggle for the preservation of the socialist system in Czechoslovakia is NOT only your task, but ours as well.

(Rhodes James, 1969 pp. 168–72)

The CCP's reply to the Warsaw Letter argued that socialism in Czechoslovakia was not under threat and strongly reaffirmed its loyalty to the USSR and to the socialist community. At the same time, the CCP made it clear that the reforms of the Action Programme would continue.

The next major development was a meeting between the Czechoslovak and Soviet leadership at Cierna-nad-Tisou (on the Czech–Soviet border) at the end of July. It was agreed – or so the Soviets understood the sense of the discussions – that Dubcek would stabilise the situation in Czechoslovakia through a clampdown on anti-communist and anti-party elements. On 3 August all the signatories of the Warsaw Letter met with Czechoslovak representatives in Bratislava, the Slovak capital, and issued a public declaration of communist solidarity and collective commitment to defend socialism in eastern Europe.

With the Bratislava Declaration, Moscow appeared to have achieved its goal of forcing the Dubcek leadership to begin a retreat from the course of reform. However, within days of the Bratislava meeting Moscow lost faith in a political solution and decided to exercise the military option of 'restoring order' in Czechoslovakia by the use of force. The decision to invade Czechoslovakia was taken at a meeting of the Soviet Politburo on 17 August. On the night of 20–1 August a combined force of twenty divisions from the five Warsaw Letter countries crossed the border into Czechoslovakia. Unlike Hungary in 1956 there was no armed struggle. Opposition to the Soviet-led invaders took the form of passive resistance and peaceful protest. Casualties were in the hundreds (including a hundred civilian deaths) rather than the thousands of the Hungarian bloodbath.

Why did Moscow abandon the search for a political solution to the Czechoslovak crisis? What appears to have happened is that Brezhnev and the other Soviet leaders lost confidence in Dubcek's willingness and ability to deliver the promises they thought he had made to them. As in the case of Hungary 1956, a crucial input shaping Moscow's perception of the situation in Czechoslovakia were the reports from Soviet representatives in the country – and these were negative as far as the likelihood of an implementation of the Cierna and Bratislava accords were concerned. As in the case of the outbreak of the Korean War, there was pressure on Moscow from other communist leaders for military action (in this instance from Gomulka and Ulbricht). As in the case of the Sino-Soviet rift, a breakdown in personal relations was an important factor in precipitating a split with erstwhile comrades. As Kieran Williams has convincingly argued (Williams articles, 1994, 1996), there was a breakdown of personal trust between the Soviet and Czechoslovak communist leaders, particularly between Brezhnev and Dubcek. The Soviet leader came to view Dubcek as insincere and dishonest, as not acting like a communist and a comrade should, appearing to say one thing but do another. If Dubcek could not be relied upon to crack down on anti-socialist and anti-Soviet elements then there were others who could be called upon to do so.

Hardline elements within the Czechoslovak communist hierarchy had been urging the Soviets to intervene for some time. It may be that the Soviets' original political goal in invading was to topple the Dubcek government and install a new, hardline regime, using the excuse that Czechoslovakia's Warsaw Pact allies had intervened to protect socialism at the invitation of these true communist elements. However, the hardliners were unable to deliver to Moscow a credible enough alternative government. The Soviets then changed tack. Having arrested Dubcek and other Czechoslovak leaders they decided to bring them to Moscow for 'negotiations'. Brezhnev told Dubcek that 'the results of the Second World War are inviolable, and we will defend them even at the cost of risking a new war' and also, quoting a Russian folk saying, said that 'without trust there is no love. And thus we have to find a solution so that there will be not only trust but mutual love as well'. Brezhnev's effort at the restoration of comradely love proved to be forlorn but he did secure a Czechoslovak–Soviet communiqué on 27 August in which Dubcek made a commitment to the 'speediest normalisation of the situation in the Czechoslovak Socialist Republic'. 'Normalisation' was code for an end to the Prague Spring and a reversion to the Soviet model of socialism and the restoration of strict communist party control of the country. Dubcek lasted in office until April 1969 when, following a series of anti-Russian popular protests, sparked off by Czechoslovakia's defeat of the USSR in the world ice hockey championships, he was replaced as party leader by the more hardline Gustav Husak. Thereafter the pace of 'normalisation' increased, including the purging in 1970 of a half million members of the communist party identified as supporters of the Prague Spring.

Following the invasion Soviet propagandists sought to put forward various justifications for the 'intervention', as they called it. The most famous of these came to be known as the 'Brezhnev Doctrine'. This was a doctrine of limited sovereignty, i.e. that the freedom of action of socialist states was limited by their obligation of loyalty to the Soviet Union and by their commitment to maintain the socialist system in their own country and to uphold the interests of the socialist community. Brezhnev's own formulation of the doctrine to which western commentators gave his name was presented at the congress of the Polish communist party in November 1968:

> When internal and external forces, hostile to socialism, seek to reverse the development of any socialist country whatsoever in the direction of the restoration of the capitalist order, when a threat to the cause of socialism arises in that country, a threat to the security of the socialist commonwealth as a whole – this already becomes not only a problem of the people of the country concerned, but also a common problem and the concern of all socialist countries.
>
> (Ashton, 1989 pp. 108–9)

Brezhnev was, of course, echoing the stance of the Warsaw Letter and, as Robert A. Jones (1990) has pointed out, the argument that the collective interests of socialism (as defined by Moscow) should override the particular interests of states, people and parties had a long pedigree in Soviet ideology. It was, for example, the justification used in support of the Soviet invasion of Hungary in 1956. The real significance of the so-called Brezhnev Doctrine was, perhaps, the fact that Moscow felt the need to offer such elaborate quasi-formal, quasi-legal justifications of the invasion at all. Part of this effort was undoubtedly aimed at quelling dissent within the world communist movement – many communist parties, in western Europe and elsewhere, had supported the Prague Spring and opposed the invasion. But Moscow's rationalisation of its actions was also aimed at the west. The message to this audience was: the Czech crisis was an internal communist affair and was resolved in accordance with the ground rules of the socialist community. There was no reason why the normalisation of east–west relations and the development of détente should be disrupted. And, essentially, the invasion of Czechoslovakia did not disrupt détente. There were western protests and some negotiations were put on hold but within a couple of years the détente of the 1970s was taking shape.

SOVIET-AMERICAN DÉTENTE, 1970–6

'After a period of confrontation, we are entering an era of negotiation,' proclaimed Richard Nixon in his inaugural speech as US President in January 1969. Two years later at the twenty-fourth congress of the CPSU in April 1971 Brezhnev unveiled a 'Peace Programme'. The programme codified previous Soviet proposals on peace, security, disarmament and the resolution of various regional conflicts. It called for an end to the Middle East and Vietnam conflicts, for collective security and the recognition of existing state boundaries in Europe, for the prohibition of weapons of mass destruction and the establishment of nuclear-free zones, for a reduction in national armed forces and the liquidation of foreign military bases, and for mutually beneficial co-operation between all states. Like all such Soviet initiatives the programme had a propagandistic intent and function. But its launch by Brezhnev was also a genuine reflection of Moscow's foreign policy priorities at this time, and was indicative of Soviet confidence in the momentum of détente that had built up since Nixon's election as president.

The starting point for the American–Soviet détente of the 1970s was the beginning of joint efforts to control the nuclear arms race. In July 1968 the USSR and the United States were the two main signatories of the Treaty on the Non-Proliferation of Nuclear Weapons – which aimed to prevent the further spread of nuclear weapons. In November 1969 the SALT (Strategic Arms Limitation Talks) negotiations began in Helsinki. In September 1971 the two sides signed a technical agreement on preventing the outbreak of an accidental nuclear war. In April 1972 came a treaty banning the development and stockpiling of biological and chemical weapons. In May 1972 the SALT negotiations resulted in an Interim Agreement which put a ceiling on the number of Soviet and American ICBMs. An Anti-Ballistic Missile (ABM) treaty which limited (to two each) the number of ABM defence systems was also signed.

(The point of this agreement was that ABM systems were considered to be destabilising in the nuclear standoff between the Soviet Union and the United States because the possibility of defending against a nuclear attack increased the temptation to use nuclear weapons.) In June 1973 the Soviet Union and the United States signed an agreement on the Prevention of Nuclear War (PNW).

These agreements were among more than two dozen Soviet–American treaties and protocols signed during the détente period. Richard Crockatt classifies these agreements into three broad categories: economic, cultural and scientific co-operation; crisis prevention and control measures; and arms control (Crockatt, 1995 p. 224). In the first category the most significant development was the Soviet–American Trade Agreement of October 1972, which provided for the granting by the US of Most Favoured Nation trading status to the USSR. (In the event the agreement foundered because of the Jackson-Vanik amendment, which tied the development of Soviet–American trade to a liberalisation of Moscow's policy on the emigration of Soviet Jews). In the category of crisis prevention there was the PNW agreement mentioned already, which provided for extensive consultation in times of international crisis. Most important there was the agreement in May 1972 on Basic Principles of Relations between the United States and the Soviet Union. The Basic Principles agreement was, as Raymond L. Garthoff put it, 'a charter for détente' (Garthoff, 1985 p. 290). It formally committed the two states to peaceful coexistence, to the avoidance of crisis and confrontation, and to the lessening of international tensions. In the field of arms control negotiations SALT 1 was followed by SALT 2 talks aimed at controlling the MIRV (multiple independent re-entry vehicles) capability of the two sides, i.e. limiting the number of deliverable nuclear warheads. Agreement on a treaty was eventually reached in June 1979. However, because of senatorial opposition the treaty was never ratified by the United States (although it was implemented in practice by the Americans).

Most of the détente agreements were signed in the glaring publicity of the Soviet–American summits of the 1970s (Brezhnev–Nixon, Moscow, May 1972; Brezhnev–Nixon, Washington, June 1973; Brezhnev–Nixon, Moscow, June 1974; Brezhnev–Ford, Vladivostok, November 1974; Brezhnev–Carter, Vienna, June 1979). But that should not obscure to us the importance of the infrastructure of the détente relationship. Most of the agreements were hammered out at subministerial level. As Nogee and Donaldson note: 'the number and variety of these agreements were unprecedented. . . . They provided for collaboration in a variety of pursuits linking the bureaucracies of both countries in endeavours never before shared' (Nogee and Donaldson, 1988 p. 270).

From Moscow's point of view at the heart of détente lay the development of political relations between the Soviet Union and the United States, expressed above all in the Basic Principles agreement (which, like the PNW agreement, was very much a Soviet initiative). Moscow believed that the political shift in superpower relations which had made détente possible had come about because of the growth in Soviet military power. The Soviet leadership was, therefore, determined *for political reasons* both to maintain strategic nuclear parity and to enhance the USSR's ability to engage in a worldwide competition for power and influence with the United States. Hence the apparently contradictory continuation of the build up of Soviet military power during the détente period. This buildup fulfilled the dual purpose of maintaining a strong defence posture while at the same time reinforcing détente. The Kremlin did not see any fundamental problem with the policy of détente and a strong defence, provided that the arms race remained controlled and the competition with the Americans took place within a stable, peaceful and cooperative framework of superpower relations. As Philip Windsor once put it, détente was seen by the Soviets as a way of making the world safe for conflict (see article by Blacker, 1983, p. 128). Moreover, as Coit D. Blacker pointed out, for Brezhnev and the Soviet leadership, détente was not a policy option but 'a fundamentally new departure in superpower relations that had been dictated by revolutionary changes in the international environment' (Blacker article, 1983 p. 120). The Soviets believed that this historic turn away from the cold war was permanent in character. Central to that conception was that the balance of forces in world politics now favoured the USSR. That appreciation of the situation was ideologically rooted in the Soviet strategy and policy of peaceful coexistence, but was more immediately founded on a pragmatic assessment of changes in the power ratio and relationship between the Soviet Union and the United States. Of some significance in this respect was the course and outcome of the Vietnam War.

There were really two wars in Vietnam. First, an anti-colonial war (1945–54) waged against France by a communist-dominated national liberation movement led by Ho Chi Minh. That war culminated in the French defeat at the battle of Dien Bien Phu in 1954. Under the July 1954 Geneva Agreements the French withdrew and the country was divided at the seventeenth parallel into a Hanoi-based northern regime controlled by Ho and the communists and a southern republic centred on Saigon backed by the Americans. As in the case of Korea the division of the country was supposed to be a temporary measure, pending all-Vietnam elections. But Washington feared that the elections would be won by Ho Chi Minh, that the whole of Vietnam would come under Hanoi's control, and that, as President Eisenhower put it, there would be a domino effect in South East Asia, with one country after another falling to the communists. Naturally, the Americans and their South Vietnamese allies stonewalled on the holding of a general election. As result the division of the country began to take on a permanent form. In response North Vietnam sponsored a rural guerrilla campaign in the south of the country. By the early 1960s the South Vietnamese government had lost control of much of the countryside. The South Vietnamese regime was dependent for its survival on American military aid. In the mid-1960s the scale of that aid increased massively, so that by 1968 there were a half million US troops in South Vietnam and American land-based and naval aircraft were bombing the North on a scale unseen since the saturation bombing of Germany and Japan in the Second World War.

Hanoi's main ally in the war was the Soviet Union. Moscow's support for North Vietnam was partly ideological, partly cold war geopolitics (i.e. anti-American) and partly the result of rivalry with China – another Hanoi ally. As well as lending diplomatic and political support, the Soviets supplied the North Vietnamese with several billion dollars worth of economic and military aid, including state-of-the-art jet fighters, bombers, anti-aircraft systems, tanks and artillery. At the same time, throughout the conflict Moscow advised Hanoi to negotiate a peace settlement with the Americans and the South Vietnamese. But, contrary to the impression in Washington, Moscow's influence on its North Vietnamese ally was limited (in this connection Hanoi was adept at threatening to play its own 'China card' as a way of fending off Soviet demands). However, in May 1968 peace negotiations did open in Paris. These finally resulted, in January 1973, in agreement on a cease-fire and the withdrawal of American forces from Vietnam. The war between the northern and southern regimes continued, however, and in April 1975 the North Vietnamese army marched into Saigon. In July 1976 the country was unified as the 'Socialist Republic of Vietnam'.

The legacy of the war for détente and Soviet foreign policy was a mixed one. On the one hand it reinforced détente. The war had complicated the détente process but it did not stop it; it showed that conflict and co-operation could coexist, provided that both sides showed restraint and sought negotiated solutions. On the other hand, the defeat of the Americans and the success of Moscow's North Vietnamese ally inflated Soviet pretensions and ambitions. As Ilya V. Gaiduk argues:

Inspired by its gains and by the decline of U.S. prestige resulting from Vietnam . . . the Soviet leadership adopted a more aggressive and rigid foreign policy, particularly in the third world. . . . Instead of seeing the U.S. defeat in Indochina as a warning against similar adventures of their own, Soviet leaders, blinded by Marxist-Leninist philosophy and by the conviction that the revolutionary trend of history was on their side, believed that where imperialism had failed they would certainly succeed . . . this belief led in the 1970s to Soviet involvement in turmoil in Africa and the Middle East and eventually to the tragedy of Afghanistan.

(Gaiduk, 1996 p. 250)

THE DECLINE OF DÉTENTE

It is conventional to date the decline of détente to 1976, the year that the Democratic Party candidate Jimmy Carter defeated Gerald Ford in the US presidential election. Under Carter there was a marked deterioration in American–Soviet relations, partly because Carter had some hawkish advisers and was under political pressure from the anti-détente lobby, and partly because he chose to make the protection of human rights (especially in the socialist countries) one of the main themes of his administration's foreign policy. But the undermining of détente had started much earlier with increasingly difficult arms control negotiations, the growth of congressional opposition to Soviet–American co-operation and with the Watergate scandal which led to Nixon's forced resignation in August 1974. Kissinger stayed on as Ford's Secretary of State, but Nixon's disgrace and departure did much to discredit and undermine détente. The defeat of Nixon's successor by Carter represented the final political denouement of the American architects of détente.

On the Soviet side, 1976 was also a key year of transition to a new, post-détente era. In that year Moscow began the deployment of the SS20s in eastern Europe – an act which did much to undermine the achievements of détente in Europe. That effect was far from being the Soviets' aim. The SS20 missiles were medium range missiles developed, it seems, with mainly China in mind, but were also deployed in Europe as a replacement for an earlier generation of IRBMs and as a means of maintaining the nuclear balance of power between NATO and the Warsaw Pact. Moscow also believed that the deployment would strengthen its bargaining position in the NATO–Warsaw Pact Mutual and Balanced Force Reduction (MBFR) talks which had begun in Vienna in 1973. In the event, NATO countered with a decision in

December 1979 to deploy, for the first time in Europe, American IRBM (Pershing) and Cruise missiles which could hit targets in the USSR, thus adding considerably to the nuclear firepower directed eastwards. Meanwhile, the prospect for a reduction in NATO-Warsaw Pact force levels receded even further.

Even more problematic for the Russians than the military consequences of the SS20 affair was the political fallout. The second half of the 1970s witnessed a sharp deterioration in Soviet–western European relations. It was, in fact, the west European members of NATO who pushed for the Pershing and Cruise deployment as a response to what was perceived as an aggressive Soviet move which by tilting the military balance in favour of the Warsaw Pact undermined the credibility of the American nuclear deterrent in Europe.

Nevertheless, Moscow persisted with its own deployment and refused to negotiate the removal of the SS20s except on the basis of compensatory reductions in nuclear forces on the western side. NATO offered the so-called zero-zero option – no SS20s and no Pershing and Cruise – but this was unacceptable to the Russians who felt they were strategically disadvantaged anyway.

There was also a series of political calculations behind Moscow's hardball tactics. First, the political gains of détente in Europe were not seen as being under threat by this dispute. Détente, remember, was viewed by Moscow as an objective and inexorable process arising out of the shifting correlation of forces. Second, Soviet foreign policy was very Amerocentric during this period and Moscow downplayed the importance of west European protests and anxieties regarding the SS20s. The Soviets also saw scope for manipulating the differences within NATO on the deployments. Third, and perhaps most important, Moscow thought it had the power to influence west European domestic politics in a favourable direction.

The mid to late 1970s was the peak of the 'Eurocommunist' challenge in west European politics. This refers to an upsurge in support for communism in western Europe. In Italy, the communist party polled 34 per cent of the vote in the 1976 general election. In France, the communists had a unity pact with François Mitterrand's Socialist Party. In 1973, this alliance won 42 per cent of the parliamentary vote and a year later Mitterrand was only just beaten by Giscard d'Estaing in the French presidential election. Following General Franco's death in 1975 the Spanish Communist Party emerged from nearly 40 years of illegality to win 10 per cent of the vote in the 1977 general election. The right-wing Greek and Portuguese dictatorships collapsed in 1974 and there too the communist parties emerged as strong contenders for a share of national political power. Other communist parties in western Europe made political gains as well. This phenomenon was labelled 'Eurocommunist' to highlight the more democratic and liberal policies and outlook of the western parties compared to their Soviet and east European counterparts (although some, including the Portuguese party, retained a more traditional outlook and remained very close to Moscow). But on the question of détente and the missile crisis there was broad communist unity. The main declaration adopted by the international Conference of Communist and Workers' Parties of Europe in June 1976 was, for example, strongly supportive of the Soviet stance on security, arms control and disarmament in Europe. In the early 1980s west European communist parties were very active in the campaign against Cruise and Pershing missiles.

To the not inconsiderable weight of the communist parties could be added the various 'peace movements' in western Europe campaigning against a further buildup of NATO military power. Some of these movements were Soviet-controlled or influenced, others were completely independent of Moscow. All contributed to the development in the late 1970s and early 1980s of a massive popular campaign in Europe against the deployment of Cruise and Pershing missiles. In Britain, for example, this was the time of the Greenham Common protests and of huge demonstrations organised by the Campaign for Nuclear Disarmament (CND).

Moscow had good reasons to believe that it had the political upperhand in the confrontation with the west over the SS20s. What Moscow did not foresee was the breakdown in the early 1980s of Soviet–American détente. In the crisis atmosphere of the new cold war the west European governments were able to resist popular protests and, in 1983, proceed with the deployment of Cruise and Pershing. At the end of the day it was apparent that the Soviets had achieved very little, except to drive west European governments further into President Reagan's anti-détente camp.

The SS20 episode complicated Soviet–American relations but it was not central to the breakdown of the superpower détente. Much more important was the impact on American opinion and perceptions of Moscow's third world policy. American anxieties centred on Soviet activities in the so-called 'arc of crisis' – an imaginary (and shifting) curved line running through countries in Africa, the Middle East and Asia. Of particular concern were the Soviet military interventions in Angola, the Horn of Africa and Afghanistan.

The Angolan intervention resulted from Soviet support for the Marxist-oriented Movement for the Popular Liberation of Angola

(MPLA). Following the collapse of Portugal's military dictatorship and of its colonial regime in Angola in 1974–5, the MPLA became involved in a civil war with American and South African-backed liberation movements. Moscow backed the MPLA both politically and with military supplies. Cuba also intervened in the conflict – sending some 17,000 combat troops to fight on behalf of the MPLA. Soviet and Cuban aid proved decisive in the MPLA victory and to the establishment of a radical, left-wing regime in Angola (a state of a 'socialist orientation' as Moscow called it). As Nogee and Donaldson comment: 'never before had communist military forces intervened so massively and decisively in Africa' (Nogee and Donaldson, 1988 p. 289). Prompting the intervention was a longstanding ideological commitment to support what Moscow saw as the legitimate national liberation movement in Angola, the logistical military capability to carry out such an action, and Cuban pressure for radical action to block American and the South African apartheid regime's moves in that country. The geopolitical context of the Soviets' continuing global rivalry with the United States was also of crucial importance. But, whatever their ideological and political ambitions, the Soviets' involvement in Angola arose out of a reaction to a developing situation rather than creation of it.

Much the same analysis is applicable to the Soviet intervention in the Horn of Africa in the mid to late 1970s. Robert G. Patman has characterised Soviet actions in that region as 'calculated opportunism' (Patman, 1990 p. xiii). A situation arose in which Moscow saw the chance of making ideological and politico-strategic gains. What happened was that in 1977–8 the Soviets and Cubans intervened in support of Ethiopia when it was attacked by neighbouring Somalia. Again, the combination of Soviet military aid and advisers and Cuban ground forces (again, about 17,000 troops) proved decisive. Ironically, defeated Somalia had previously been a Soviet and Cuban ally but the Somalis had broken with Moscow and Havana when refused support in the territorial disputes with Ethiopia about the status of the Ogaden and Eritrea. Indeed, Moscow's preferred option in the Horn was a political settlement which would enable it to maintain alliances with both Somalia and Ethiopia. Instead, the war meant that the relationship with Somalia was severed and the Soviets were left with Ethiopia, which was governed by a left-wing military dictatorship. Through its intervention Moscow lost one but gained another 'socialist' ally in Africa, as well as useful port facilities for its growing 'blue water' navy. But, again, these natural, opportunistic developments were hardly evidence of a programme of Soviet aggression and expansionism.

The Soviet military intervention in Afghanistan, which began in

1979–80, is in a somewhat different category from those in Angola and Ethiopia. This was a Soviet war, the invasion and military occupation by the USSR of a neighbouring state, which during the course of nine years cost the lives of at least 15,000 Soviet soldiers, and left hundreds of thousands of Afghans dead and wounded. Conceived as a quick and decisive military operation, which would be followed by a rapid withdrawal of Soviet forces, the intervention in Afghanistan became the USSR's Vietnam.

The origins of the war dated back to April 1978 when a left-wing military coup in Kabul brought to power the People's Democratic Party of Afghanistan (PDPA), an umbrella organisation of the two factions of the Afghani communist movement, the Khalq and the Parcham. In the internal political struggle which followed the Khalq faction triumphed. The key figure was Hafizullah Amin, who in March 1979 became first Prime Minister and then, after murdering the incumbent (another communist), President in October 1979.

The new socialist government pursued a policy of the radical reform of Afghan society and culture, which brought it into direct conflict with many supporters of Islam, some of whom took up arms against the new regime. During 1978–9 there developed a civil war in Afghanistan between the Kabul government and Muslim insurgents. Amin appealed to Moscow for military assistance. The Soviets, who had signed a friendship treaty with Afghanistan in December 1978, were willing to continue sending supplies and military advisers but they held back from more direct military intervention (although some army units were dispatched to protect key communication and transportation networks). Moscow urged a political solution on Amin: a slowing down of the reform programme, efforts to win popular support among the Muslim masses, and Khalq–Parcham communist unity in the face of the common enemy.

The situation in Afghanistan continued to deteriorate, however. By December 1979 Soviet leaders had reached two conclusions: first, that Amin had to be deposed and, second, that a direct, large-scale deployment of Soviet forces was necessary to quell the popular armed revolt in Afghanistan. On Christmas Day 1979 Soviet airborne troops landed in Kabul. Two days later the paras with the assistance of the KGB attacked Amin's presidential palace, and captured and executed the Afghan leader. Meanwhile, Soviet ground forces had crossed the border into Afghanistan. In all 85,000 Soviet troops in 7 divisions were involved in the initial invasion.

The new Soviet-installed President of Afghanistan was Babrak Karmal, the leader of the Parcham faction. The Soviet aim was to quash the Islamic insurgency and stabilise the political situation under the rule of the new government.

A variety of motives informed the decision to intervene militarily. Moscow was concerned to preserve a left-wing regime in Afghanistan and avoid the destabilising danger of a fundamentalist Muslim regime on its border which might provoke trouble among Soviet Islamic peoples. An important part of the background in this respect was the popular revolution in neighbouring Iran in 1979 which had overthrown the Shah's regime and replaced it with a fundamentalist Islamic state which was very much dedicated to the further spread of Muslim ideology (a point that would not have escaped Moscow's attention). The loss of Afghanistan would, moreover, have been a setback for Soviet international prestige and would have undermined communist confidence in the onward march of socialism. As ever there was a personal element, too. The Soviets fell out with Amin, felt soiled by his murderous factional activities and became increasingly receptive to dissident voices within the PDPA. Undoubtedly, too, there was a calculation that the Soviet armed forces would be able to secure a rapid and decisive victory over the Afghan guerrillas. That turned out to be a major miscalculation as the Soviets found themselves drawn into a costly, ignominious and losing war of attrition. (On Afghanistan, see the articles by Westad, 1994 and 1996–7b.)

The possible impact on détente of the Afghanistan intervention does not appear to have played a major part in internal Soviet deliberations. Discussions tended to focus on the internal situation in Afghanistan rather than possible international ramifications (although there was some concern that Amin might rapidly switch to a western orientation in foreign policy). The same narrow focus was evident in the next crisis to dominate Moscow's foreign policy agenda: the Solidarity crisis in Poland in 1980–1.

'Solidarity' was an independent trade union-cum-political movement that emerged in summer 1980 in the wake of protests and strikes against government imposed increases in food prices. The strikers, based in the shipyards of Gdansk, forced the government to rescind the price increases and to sign an accord in August 1980 recognising Solidarity's rights as a free trade union. This marked the beginning of a long-drawn-out struggle for power between the communist party and the rapidly growing Solidarity which, with the support of the Catholic Church, increasingly sought to challenge the communist order in Poland.

In Moscow, Solidarity's battles with the communist authorities were viewed as part of a process of creeping counter-revolution that would lead to the end of socialism in Poland. In 1980, as in 1956, the end of socialism in Poland and the loss of Poland as a Soviet ally and a member of the Warsaw Pact was completely unacceptable to Moscow. 'We simply cannot and must not lose Poland,' Foreign Minister Gromyko told the Politburo in October 1980 (Kramer article, 1995 p. 118). The option to invade and crush Solidarity by force was considered seriously and at length in Moscow. Detailed plans for such a military operation were drawn up. Communist leaders in Bulgaria, Czechoslovakia and the GDR supported a military solution. But the military option was eventually rejected. As one Politburo member put it, 'if troops are introduced that will be a catastrophe'. Poland was not Czechoslovakia in 1968 or even Hungary in 1956. Poland was the largest country in eastern Europe, with a population of more than 30 million. It was a country of strong anti-Russian and anti-Soviet traditions and currently had a mass, mobilised anti-communist movement. An invasion of Poland would mean a Polish–Soviet war, and the Russians were already having enough trouble in Afghanistan. Instead, Moscow opted to push for an internal political solution. This took the form of the introduction of martial law in December 1981 by Poland's new communist leader, General Wojciech Jaruzelski. Martial law and the arrest of Solidarity's leaders was welcomed with much relief in Moscow.

Although calculations regarding détente were not in the forefront of Moscow's decision-making during the Polish crisis, they were not entirely absent. There was a recognition that the changes in international relations in the 1970s had created a new set of constraints on Moscow's freedom of action. This awareness surfaced at the critical meeting of the Politburo in December 1981. M.A. Suslov, the head of the Politburo's special commission on the Polish crisis, noted:

> We've done a great deal of work for peace, and it is now impossible for us to change our position. World public opinion will not permit us to do so. We have carried out via the UN such momentous diplomatic actions to consolidate peace. What great effect we have had from the visit of L.I. Brezhnev to the FRG and from many other peaceful actions we have undertaken. This has enabled all peace-loving countries to understand that the Soviet union staunchly and consistently upholds a policy of peace. That is why it is now impossible for us to change the position we have adopted vis-à-vis Poland since the very start of the Polish events.
>
> (Kramer article, 1995 p. 137)

Moscow may have felt it was acting with restraint, but the imposition of martial law in Poland was yet another blow to the faltering east–west détente. By the early 1980s détente was in deep trouble. Soviet–American and Soviet–west European relations were increasingly captive to the new cold war rhetoric of Ronald Reagan, Margaret Thatcher and other hawkish western politicians. Backing up the Reaganite rhetoric was a near doubling of American defence spending, an explicit return to the cold war policy of negotiating with the Russians from 'positions of strength' and the implementation of economic sanctions against the USSR as punishment for acts of aggression (for example, after the introduction of martial law in Poland). Moscow was also faced with the so-called 'Reagan Doctrine'. In October 1983 Reagan proclaimed that 'the goal of the free world must no longer be stated in the negative, that is, resistance to Soviet expansionism. The goal of the free world must instead be stated in the affirmative. We must go on the offensive with a forward strategy for freedom'. In practice, the doctrine meant American material and political support for armed 'freedom fighters' in various countries, including Afghanistan where the guerrillas received $2 billion in US aid. To the Soviets the doctrine was an American 'neoglobalist' strategy which aimed to wear down the USSR and its allies in the third world.

Even in Moscow they began to have doubts about détente as it became increasingly clear that the period of negotiation had given way to a new era of confrontation. In his last public pronouncement on foreign policy in October 1982 Brezhnev stated that 'the ruling circles of the United States of America have launched a political, ideological and economic offensive on socialism and have raised the intensity of their military preparations to an unprecedented level'. Yuri Andropov, Brezhnev's successor as party leader, was initially optimistic about the prospects for détente. In November 1982 he told the party central committee:

> We are deeply convinced that the Seventies, characterised by détente, were not – as is asserted by some imperialist figures – a chance episode in the difficult history of mankind. No, the policy of détente is by no means a past stage. The future belongs to it.

A year later, however, the mood in Moscow had shifted. In a keynote address on the sixty-sixth anniversary of the Bolshevik Revolution, Politburo member Grigorii Romanov declared that 'the international situation at present is white hot . . . perhaps never before in the postwar decades has the atmosphere in the world been as tense as it is now.' But when Andropov died and was succeeded by Konstantin Chernenko as Soviet leader in February 1984, the pendulum swung back in the favour of a more positive attitude to the prospects for détente. 'The USSR will fully cooperate', he told the central committee, 'with all states which are prepared to assist through practical deeds to reduce international tension and to create an atmosphere of trust in the world.' A year later, however, Chernenko himself was dead. It was left to his successor as Soviet leader, Mikhail Gorbachev, to pursue the renewal of détente.

5 From coexistence to collaboration
The Gorbachev revolution, 1985–91

A new way of thinking is not an improvisation,
nor a mental exercise. It is a result of serious
reflections on the realities of today's world,
of the understanding that a responsible attitude
to policy demands scientific substantiation, and
that some of the postulates which seemed
unshakable before should be given up. . . . And we
draw inspiration from Lenin. Turning to him . . .
one is struck by his ability to get at the root
of things, to see the most intricate dialectics
of world processes. . . . More than once he spoke
about the priority of interests common to all
humanity over class interests. It is only now that
we have come to comprehend the entire depth and
significance of these ideas. It is they that are
feeding our philosophy of international relations,
and the new way of thinking.
(M.S. Gorbachev, November 1987)

OVERVIEW

A major theme of this book has been the importance of the doctrinal context of Soviet thinking on international relations and how shifts in ideology have sometimes resulted in radical changes in foreign policy. The Soviet declaration of the cold war, Khrushchev's competitive coexistence, Brezhnev's pursuit of détente – all were ideology driven to an important degree. Under Mikhail Gorbachev there was an intellectual revolution in the USSR which transformed Soviet ideology and revolutionised the character of the Soviet Union's domestic politics and foreign policy. The final, unintended outcome of this revolutionary transformation was the end of communist party rule in the Soviet

Union, the abolition of the socialist system, and the disintegration of the USSR. When Gorbachev left office in December 1991 the Soviet Union had ceased to exist as an actor in world politics, its place taken by the multitude of states which had emerged from the implosion of the USSR.

The destruction of Soviet communism and the Soviet state was far from being Gorbachev's aim when he came to power in 1985. On the contrary, his goal was to revitalise the Soviet system and to strengthen the USSR's role and influence in world affairs. To achieve this Gorbachev pursued 'perestroika' (reconstruction), 'glasnost' (openness) and 'Novoe Myshlenie' (New Thinking). Perestroika referred to Gorbachev's goal of a fundamental reform of the Soviet economic system. Glasnost was the slogan that summed up Gorbachev's liberalisation and democratisation of the Soviet political system. New Thinking referred to Gorbachev's rethinking of the traditional principles, concepts and goals of Soviet foreign policy.

Gorbachev's New Thinking on Soviet foreign policy represented a break with the 'old thinking' of the previous communist regime but there was considerable continuity as well. During his first years in power Gorbachev's aim was, like that of Andropov and Chernenko before him, the resumption of peaceful coexistence and détente with the west. Where he differed from his predecessors was that to achieve this goal he was willing to give up what had previously been considered by Moscow to be vital foreign policy interests. Distinctive, too, was Gorbachev's ideological and strategic vision of the purposes of détente: not world socialism, but peace, international co-operation and the long-term coexistence of systems with convergent rather than conflicting values and outlooks. In effect, Gorbachev de-ideologised Soviet foreign policy by detaching peaceful coexistence from the revolutionary ideology and politics that had given birth to it after the Russian Revolution.

Gorbachev's new version of peaceful coexistence was vital to the achievement of a renewed détente with the United States and western Europe in 1985–8. However, it was not until the events of 1989 in eastern Europe that the full radical implications of Gorbachev's new foreign policy became apparent. In 1989 the communist regimes of Bulgaria, Czechoslovakia, the GDR, Hungary, Poland and Romania collapsed. The conditions for this collapse were created by Gorbachev's encouragement and support for radical political reform in eastern Europe. It was Gorbachev's repudiation of the Brezhnev Doctrine and his willingness to give up Soviet control of eastern Europe which made possible the rapid and relatively peaceful transition to post-communism in the region.

The cold war had begun with the postwar division of Europe. It quickly and conclusively came to an end with the disintegration of the eastern bloc. Symbolically the most important sign of the end of the cold war was the fall of the Berlin Wall in November 1989 and the reunification of Germany a year later. While Germany remained in NATO, the cold war institutions of the former Soviet–east European bloc were crumbling. In 1991 both the Warsaw Pact and the Council for Mutual Economic Assistance (CMEA) were abolished.

Gorbachev's increasingly radical course internationally in the mid-1980s was paralleled by the policies he pursued at home. An initially moderate programme of economic and political reform had metamorphosised by 1989–90 into the goal of effecting a transition from authoritarian communism to a western-style democracy with a social market (rather than a socialist economic) system which combined a welfare state with a mixture of private and public enterprise.

The problem was that Gorbachev's drive for radical reform undermined (in part, intentionally as Gorbachev strove to establish for himself a new, democratic political base) the communist party – the only institution capable of running the country while the heavily centralised Soviet system remained in being; deepening economic crisis and political chaos were the result of a loss of communist party control of the system. Glasnost introduced free speech and political pluralism into the Soviet system, but it also facilitated the emergence and growing challenge of various national and ethnic groups in the USSR which, having been subsumed in communism and the Soviet system, were now striving for independence and self-expression (often at the expense of minorities in their own lands). Gorbachev moved to head off the nationalist challenge, at first by amending the Soviet Constitution and then by introducing a new Union Treaty which would grant more power and decision-making to the constituent Republics of the USSR – thereby creating a Union of *Sovereign* Soviet Republics. That initiative was undermined by a coup attempt in August 1991 by hardliners within the Gorbachev government opposed to the new Union Treaty as well as other aspects of the radical version of perestroika and glasnost being pursued at the time. The coup failed, but in its aftermath Boris Yeltsin, President of the Russian Republic, and the leaders of other Soviet Republics asserted their independence. Gorbachev soon found himself the leader of an entity – the USSR – which for all practical purposes had ceased to exist. He resigned as Soviet leader on 25 December 1991.

GORBACHEV'S NEW THINKING ON SOVIET FOREIGN POLICY

Gorbachev was elected General Secretary of the party in March 1985. The first sign of a radical rethinking of foreign policy came (privately) at a meeting of the central committee in April 1985. At that meeting (the April Plenum, as it later became known) Gorbachev spoke about reactivating arms control negotiations; the withdrawal of Soviet troops from Afghanistan; devising a new military-strategic doctrine based on the criteria of 'reasonable sufficiency'; and about the development of 'civilised' as well as peaceful relations between states.

The first major public statement of New Thinking on Soviet foreign policy was delivered by Gorbachev a year later at the twenty-seventh party congress in February 1986. Gorbachev's main theme was global interdependence. He argued that all states had common economic, environmental and security problems which they had to deal with collectively on the basis of common interests and common human values. Gorbachev spoke of an 'integral' rather than divided world and moved away from the concept of peaceful coexistence as a form of class struggle and as a strategy for socialism. (The latter formulation of the policy of peaceful coexistence was deleted from a new edition of the party programme agreed at the congress.)

Gorbachev also emphasised that 'the task of insuring [national] security is a political task and can be resolved only by political means'. Linked to this view was the idea that national defence should be based on reasonable military sufficiency; the superiority of enemy forces did not matter as long as you had sufficient counter-force to deter any attack, including a nuclear one. To an extent Gorbachev was returning to the doctrine prevalent in Khrushchev's time, which had been an era of US strategic superiority. The post-Khrushchev pursuit of military parity had partly been a matter of a change in military doctrine but it also embodied, as we have seen, the political calculation that the possibility of détente and peaceful coexistence rested on Soviet military power. It was this doctrine that Gorbachev decisively repudiated. Soviet security would be safeguarded primarily through political co-operation and negotiations, and détente would be attained by reason and political persuasion, not military might. It was an astonishing idea for any politician to embrace, and even more extraordinary for a leader of the Soviet Union. It indicated a perception of the outside world, particularly of the west and its political leaders that was very different from previous generations of Soviet leaders.

After the twenty-seventh congress Gorbachev further developed the

New Thinking in a series of speeches, articles and books. The break with traditional Soviet ideology became more and more pronounced. By the end of his reign the language and ideas of Gorbachev's foreign policy had more in common with western liberalism and humanism than with the socialism and Marxism-Leninism of his Kremlin predecessors.

Another aspect of the New Thinking, which was very much linked to glasnost, was the development of a public discussion and critique of the historical record of Soviet foreign policy. The central committee's theses for the nineteenth party conference, which opened on 28 June 1988, criticised Soviet foreign during the Brezhnev years for its 'subjectivism' and 'dogmatism'. Thereafter, many past foreign actions of the USSR came under scrutiny and the old Soviet leadership was often found wanting. These discussions were incorporated into official discourse and policy. The invasion of Czechoslovakia was, for example, repudiated as a misconceived and illegal act. Historians were given more and more access to the secrets tucked away in Soviet archives. It became permissible to criticise current as well as past Soviet foreign policy. By the late 1980s discussion of international affairs in the Soviet Union was as free and diverse as in any country. It should be noted in this context that while Gorbachev's foreign policies were enormously popular abroad, at home they encountered strong criticism and opposition from a variety of different points of view.

Where did Gorbachev's ideas come from? One answer to this question is that they came from the west, particularly from the liberal and social democratic political traditions. That is true, but there were other sources as well. One of these was, surprisingly, Soviet ideology itself, which contained many elements which Gorbachev and his supporters were able to draw upon and emphasise in support of glasnost, perestroika and the New Thinking. Gorbachev's strong commitment to peace, co-operation and détente, for example, was straight out of the mainstream Soviet ideological tradition. His talk of democracy, popular participation, and the integrity and importance of the individual was common parlance in Soviet political discourse (the problem was not the theory but the practice). Then there was the personal and biographical factor. Gorbachev was of the generation (b. 1931) which came of political age in the 1950s, at the time of Khrushchev's attempted destalinisation and liberalisation of the Soviet Union. In many respects the first years of Gorbachev's rule were a reprise of that earlier era of reform. It is also important to remember that Gorbachev was not the first communist leader to radically revise his ideology. There were many, many precedents. In recent times, Dubcek and the communist reformers of the Prague Spring had trod the path of ideological revision in

1968. Glasnost and perestroika bore an uncanny resemblance to the Action Programme of the Czechoslovak Communist Party. In the 1970s the Eurocommunist leaders of the west European communist parties had pioneered much of the critique of traditional communist and Marxist ideology which Gorbachev was to embrace in the 1980s. In the Soviet Union itself there had always been an undercurrent of communist dissent from the party orthodoxy. This reform tradition in the communist movement was an important part of the background to the Gorbachev era and an important political and ideological influence on Gorbachev himself.

There were also a series of more pragmatic and immediate reasons prompting Gorbachev's New Thinking. First, the failure of the 1970s détente and the renewal of the cold war in the 1980s demanded a new approach in Soviet foreign policy if the dangerous confrontation with the US was to be ended. Second, by the mid-1980s the USSR was suffering from what might be loosely called 'imperial overstretch' – its global competition with the US, involvements in the third world, and the war in Afghanistan were a drain on national resources the country could ill afford at a time when Gorbachev was striving to radically restructure the economy. Foreign policy needed to facilitate Soviet disengagement from various theatres of competition and conflict. Third, the stagnant Soviet economy (and the ailing socialist economies of eastern Europe) needed an injection of technological and developmental dynamism that could only come from the west. Détente and the elimination of barriers to east–west trade were seen as a necessary condition of Soviet economic revival. Finally, there was also the degree to which Gorbachev's radical foreign policies were a substitute for failed domestic policies and a means of deflecting criticism from political opponents at home. Like all Soviet leaders, Gorbachev discovered that it was much easier to direct foreign policy and influence world political developments than to control the domestic situation.

It is important to remember, too, that the New Thinking and its practical application in Soviet foreign policy developed gradually and in response to a variety of changing circumstances. There was a detailed story to Soviet foreign policy under Gorbachev as well as a grand theme and a final, dramatic outcome. Neither was it just Gorbachev's story. Gorbachev's leadership of Soviet foreign policy was as strong and decisive as any of his predecessors, including Stalin. But there were other important advocates and practitioners of the New Thinking, most notably Eduard Shevardnadze, Gorbachev's Foreign Minister. Shevardnadze's appointment as Gromyko's replacement in July 1985 was one of Gorbachev's first and most important acts of foreign policy. Gromyko had been Foreign Minister since 1957 and was very much a figure of the old regime. He had been one of the architects of the 1970s détente, but was also closely identified with its weaknesses and failures (particularly the reliance on military power). He was not the man to front up the 'peace offensive' launched by Gorbachev in mid-1985.

THE CREATION OF A NEW DÉTENTE, 1985–8

Even before Gorbachev came to power there had been signs of a possible improvement in Soviet–American relations. Now into its second term, the Reagan administration began to soften its stance on the Soviet Union. Early in 1985 agreement was reached on the resumption of arms control negotiations, which had stalled following a Soviet walkout of the talks in November 1983.

Gorbachev quickly moved to take the initiative in the arms control arena. In April 1985 he froze further deployments of the SS20s (and six months later announced a reduction in the number of deployed missiles). In August 1985 he declared a unilateral moratorium (temporary halt) to Soviet underground nuclear testing. In September 1985 he proposed that the USSR and the US reduce their strategic nuclear weapons arsenals by 50 per cent.

All these initiatives were curtain-raisers for the American–Soviet summit in Geneva in November 1985. The summit achieved little by way of concrete agreements, but it was the first such summit in six years and it did reinvigorate the Soviet–American political and strategic dialogue. Importantly, it was the start of a constructive personal relationship between Gorbachev and Reagan. It also became apparent at the summit that Gorbachev's personal and public style were very different from that of his predecessors. Here was a Soviet leader capable of charming the media and beating the Americans in the public relations war for the support of international public opinion. The Geneva summit marked the beginning of Gorbachev's rise to the status of the most popular and trusted statesman in the world. His approval ratings in the US soared way above those of US politicians. By the end of the 1980s he was *Time* magazine's Man of the Decade. A poll conducted by *The European* newspaper in 1989 revealed that he was west European voters' choice as the President of a United Europe. In 1990 he was awarded the Nobel Peace Prize.

The Soviet peace offensive continued after the Geneva summit. In January 1986 Gorbachev proposed the elimination of all nuclear weapons in the world by the year 2000. In April 1986 he offered new negotiations on the reduction of NATO and Warsaw Pact conventional forces. In October 1986 he met Reagan again, this time in Reykjavik. This summit was more acrimonious than Geneva, mainly because of the 'Star Wars' controversy.

In March 1983 Reagan had announced the Strategic Defence Initiative (SDI – popularly called Star Wars because of the motion picture of the same name which featured laser weapon battles in space). This was a plan for nuclear and laser-armed satellites which would destroy ballistic missiles launched into the atmosphere. Reagan claimed that such a missile defence system would nullify the threat of nuclear weapons (at least of the ballistic kind) and make the world a safer place. MAD (Mutually Assured Destruction) would be replaced by SAD (Strategically Assured Defence).

The Soviets (including Gorbachev) viewed SDI less benevolently. They saw the Star Wars research programme as a violation of the 1972 ABM treaty which limited the development and deployment of missile defence systems. They saw it as an escalation of the arms race, as introducing nuclear weapons into space – weapons which could be used for offensive as well as defensive purposes. The worst case scenario was that Star Wars would make the US invulnerable to nuclear retaliation and encourage an American nuclear strike on the USSR (this was, remember, the Reagan era). The Soviets feared that this was one scientific and technological race that the USSR would not be able to keep up with. At the same time, Moscow ridiculed the idea of Star Wars and argued that it was scientifically and technologically unfeasible (which rather undermined the fuss made about SDI's threat to world peace).

At Reykjavik Gorbachev and Reagan agreed that strategic nuclear weapons should be cut by 50 per cent and the Soviet and American medium range missiles in Europe would be withdrawn. But the summit broke up without agreement because Reagan refused to back down on SDI and because Gorbachev insisted on tying other arms control agreements to an abandonment of the Star Wars project. The deadlock proved to be short-lived, however. A few months later, in February 1987, Gorbachev announced that he was prepared to resolve the east–west dispute over the deployment of the SS20s and the Pershing/Cruise missiles in Europe on the basis of the NATO policy of zero–zero – the withdrawal by both sides of their missiles. This radical change in Soviet policy paved the way for the Washington summit of December 1987 at which the Intermediate Nuclear Forces (INF) treaty was signed. Under the terms of the INF treaty all intermediate and shorter range missiles deployed in Europe were withdrawn. For the first time arms control negotiations had resulted in the elimination of a whole category of missiles and in an actual reduction of nuclear arsenals (albeit only 5 per cent of the world's 50,000 nuclear warheads at that time).

In signing the INF treaty Gorbachev had reversed a Soviet policy of ten years' standing and had accepted a compromise based on terms laid down by the west. This was to become a pattern in Soviet foreign policy under Gorbachev: breaking logjams in arms control and political negotiations by accepting compromises based on western proposals and wishes. (Gorbachev's critics at home characterised these 'compromises' as surrenders).

Unilateral Soviet initiatives to create a new détente also continued to come thick and fast. One of the most important was Gorbachev's announcement in February 1988 of a Soviet military withdrawal from Afghanistan. In April an international agreement on ending foreign involvement in the Afghan civil war was signed in Geneva. By February 1989 the last of the 100,000 Soviet army that had occupied and fought in Afghanistan for nearly ten years had been withdrawn.

One of the most notable spinoffs of the Afghanistan withdrawal was that it paved the way for a healing of the Sino-Soviet rift. A Soviet withdrawal from Afghanistan had been a key Chinese precondition for the betterment of Sino-Soviet relations. (Others included a reduction of Soviet forces along the Sino-Soviet border and the withdrawal of Vietnamese troops from Cambodia – which had invaded that country (a Chinese ally) in 1978/9.) In May 1989 a summit in Beijing between Gorbachev and the Chinese leadership declared a normalisation of Sino-Soviet relations. Relations between the two communist parties were also restored. One of the more remarkable aspects of the summit was that Gorbachev's arrival in Beijing was greeted by hundreds of thousands of students who, inspired by glasnost and perestroika in Russia, demanded democracy in China. The day after the Soviet leader's departure the Chinese government declared martial law and then used massive military force to clear, violently and with much loss of life, the demonstrators from Tiananmen Square.

The Soviet withdrawal from Afghanistan was a special case of what Raymond L. Garthoff has called the 'Gorbachev Doctrine' (Garthoff, 1994 p. 734). This was a policy of disengagement from third world conflicts via the sponsorship of peaceful resolution of armed struggles and political disputes, preferably on the basis of local and regional democratisation. Moscow's partner in this endeavour – in Africa, Asia and South America, in country after country – was the United States. As Garthoff says:

The Gorbachev Doctrine represented a shift of policy and performance, disengaging by choice from the whole global confrontation with the United States, to a policy predicated on cooperative security and normalised relations with other countries. By the end of the Gorbachev (and Soviet) eras, the Soviet Union and the United States had indeed become global partners to a degree that was unthinkable just a few years earlier.

(Garthoff, 1994 p. 748)

As Garthoff indicates, one of the dynamics of the change in Soviet third world policy was the desire to avoid entanglements which complicated and undermined the growing détente relationship with the US – a consideration that Soviet leaders before Gorbachev tended to downgrade in importance. Another factor was a calculation of the political and economic costs and benefits of Soviet involvement in third world conflicts. But alongside this there was also an important ideological reappraisal of Soviet strategy. Having abandoned the ideology of national liberation and world revolution there was very little incentive for the Soviets to continue backing radical movements and regimes in the third world, especially when it was now possible to negotiate the withdrawal of American support for right-wing and reactionary 'freedom fighters'.

The Gorbachev Doctrine also reflected the focusing of Soviet security concerns on Europe as well as on relations with the United States. One of the early themes of Gorbachev's New Thinking was that the Soviet Union, eastern Europe and western Europe shared a 'common European home', extending, as De Gaulle had put it, from the Atlantic to the Urals. The continent of Europe (including Russia) was in many ways, he argued, a single entity, with a common history, culture, traditions and values. European countries had common problems, particularly in the field of security, which could only be resolved on a common basis. There was, he said, a need for pan-European initiatives which broke down the artificial, cold war barriers dividing the continent.

In 1989 those barriers were broken down, but not in the way envisaged by Gorbachev, or anyone else for that matter.

THE FALL OF COMMUNISM IN EASTERN EUROPE, 1989

Gorbachev's policy of glasnost and perestroika was a programme for the reform of eastern Europe as well as the Soviet Union. Local reform initiatives in east European countries were encouraged by Moscow, and

Gorbachev welcomed rather than feared the growing expectations of people in eastern Europe that they too would get the freedom and democracy increasingly available to Soviet citizens.

The official response in the Eastern bloc to the Gorbachev reforms was mixed. In Poland and Hungary the communists embraced the opportunity for change.

In Poland in January 1989 Solidarity – banned since the introduction of martial law in 1981 – was legalised. By April Solidarity and the Polish communist government had negotiated an agreement on political and economic reform, including the holding of (freeish) elections. The elections were held in June and won convincingly by Solidarity. In August 1989 the Polish Parliament elected the first non-communist Prime Minister in eastern Europe in over 40 years.

In Hungary, the equivalent of glasnost and perestroika had been underway for some time, but the pace of political reform really began to accelerate when the communists agreed to the introduction of multiparty elections (a promise that was implemented in 1990). Recall, that in 1956 the Soviets had invaded Hungary precisely in order to avert such a development.

Elsewhere in eastern Europe – in Bulgaria, Czechoslovakia, the GDR and Romania – there was retrenchment in the face of the Gorbachev challenge. Indeed, substantial efforts were made to insulate the local population from the subversive ideas coming out of the Soviet Union! There were, nonetheless, murmurings of popular discontent, particularly in Czechoslovakia where there was a revival of interest in the ideas of the Prague Spring, but there was no sign of a major challenge to the power of the communist authorities. The dissidents remained a small minority, very much on the fringes of politics and power. Then, in September 1989, the GDR entered a period of intense crisis that was to end with a complete remaking of the political map of Europe.

The East German crisis was sparked off by Hungary's decision in August 1989 to open its border with Austria. This opened a route to the west for GDR citizens wishing to emigrate to the FRG (there was no wall dividing Hungary and East Germany). Thousands of East Germans crossed the border into Hungary en route to Austria and the FRG. Eric Honecker, the GDR communist leader, was faced with a crisis similar to that which had confronted his predecessor Walter Ulbricht at the time of the building of the Berlin Wall: the possible collapse of the East German economy as a result of mass emigration and a perhaps fatal sapping of the regime's political moral. Unlike Ulbricht, Honecker could not rely on Soviet support or the threat of Soviet military action to resolve the crisis. Indeed, when Gorbachev visited East

Berlin in October on the occasion of the fortieth anniversary of the founding of the GDR he urged Honecker to urgently introduce political reforms. 'Life punishes latecomers,' he told Honecker. The news of Gorbachev's representations encouraged pro-democracy demonstrations in Leipzig and other East German cities. On 18 October Honecker resigned as party leader. By the end of October the GDR population was demonstrating in its hundreds of thousands, demanding, among other things, the right to emigrate. On 4 November there was a half million strong demonstration in East Berlin. On 7 November the communist government resigned. On 8 November Egon Krenze, Honecker's successor as leader of the communist party, took the decision to open the Berlin Wall.

In Bulgaria and Czechoslovakia there were similar mass, popular, peaceful uprisings, which drew much inspiration from events in the GDR. The communist governments resigned there, too. The communist regimes in all three countries were replaced by democratic multi-party political systems on western lines. In Czechoslovakia the long-time dissident Vaclav Haval became president of the country, while Alexander Dubcek also came in from the cold and was elected chairman of the federal parliament.

Events in Romania took a somewhat different course. There, the communist leader Nicolae Ceauşescu and his supporters strongly resisted popular demands for political change. In December there were violent clashes between demonstrators and the security forces. On 22 December the Romanian army launched an anti-Ceauşescu coup. A shoot-out between the army and the security forces ensued. The Ceauşescu supporters lost and, on 25 December, the Romanian leader and his wife were captured and executed.

At the height of the fighting in Bucharest the US Secretary of State James Baker said that Washington would not object if the Soviet Union intervened militarily against Ceauşescu. Moscow, however, was pursing a strict policy of non-intervention in relation to events in eastern Europe – except to welcome the prospects for reform and democratisation. At the height of the East German crisis the Soviet press spokesman, Gennady Gerasimov, is said to have quipped that the Brezhnev Doctrine had been replaced by the 'Sinatra Doctrine' – they could do it their way! A more formal declaration of non-interference in east European internal affairs had been issued by a Warsaw Pact meeting on 27 October.

Gorbachev hoped that 'their way' would be a reform of socialism in eastern Europe and the refoundation of the socialist community on a new, open and democratic basis. In 1989 the political future of eastern

Europe was still not entirely clear, apart from an end to the old communist regimes. Also beyond doubt was the end of Soviet control in eastern Europe. Gorbachev had given up one of the foundation-stones of postwar Soviet security. In part this had been a matter of pragmatics and politics. There wasn't much Moscow could have done to alter the course events took. The use of or threat of force was not an option in the age of glasnost and perestroika, even had Moscow wished to exercise such an option to prop up hardline anti-Gorbachev regimes. Of importance, too, was Gorbachev's redefinition of Soviet security needs, which downgraded the importance of a political-military bloc in Europe. But, most importantly, Soviet non-intervention was the result of a political conviction, not least on Gorbachev's part, that people had the right to decide their own futures, even if that meant the end of communism and of the Soviet sphere of influence in eastern Europe.

THE END OF THE COLD WAR AND THE END OF THE USSR, 1990–1

Gorbachev's conversion to the principles of democracy, self-determination and sovereignty in eastern Europe did not mean that he had forgone the right to negotiate about Soviet interests and concerns. An important case in point was the question of the future of the GDR after the fall of the Wall. At first, Gorbachev resisted the movement towards German reunification. The idea that a divided (and therefore weaker) Germany was a safeguard for Soviet security remained strong in Moscow. The extension of NATO eastwards was also a matter of some concern. But Gorbachev eventually gave in to western pressure on this matter and in September 1990 German unity was agreed by Moscow provided that there was a reduction of the German army and that no NATO forces were stationed in the territory of the former GDR. There was also provision for financial support for the withdrawal of Soviet forces from East Germany. By this time negotiations were also underway on Soviet troop withdrawals from other East bloc countries.

Gorbachev and George Bush had declared the cold war over at the Malta summit in December 1989. 'We don't consider you an enemy any more', Gorbachev told the US President. The agreement on German reunification was further practical proof of this assertion. Other important developments included the signing of a treaty on the reduction of Conventional Forces in Europe (CFE) in November 1990 and serious negotiations on reductions in nuclear weapons. In July 1991 the START treaty was signed in Moscow. This provided for significant reductions in the Soviet and American strategic nuclear arsenals. (In 1993 a START 2 treaty was signed by Russia and the United States.)

One of the most significant signs of the new relationship between Moscow and Washington was Soviet support for the Americans in the Gulf War of 1990–1 – in spite of the fact that Iraq was a long-time Middle East ally of the USSR. While at various points during the war the Soviets attempted to mediate an Iraqi withdrawal from Kuwait, there was no doubting their basic solidarity with the American (and UN) position. After the war the Soviet Union was joint sponsor of a peace conference on the Arab–Israeli dispute which opened in Madrid in October 1991.

Gorbachev's foreign policy during this period was not without its critics at home. The loss of eastern Europe, the reduction of Soviet military power, the abandonment of Iraq, and what was seen as Gorbachev's general kowtowing to the Americans – these were all objects of hardline criticism, including within his own administration.

The coup plotters of August 1991 were mainly concerned about the danger of a break up of the USSR following the introduction of a new Union treaty, but their dissatisfaction with what they saw as the international decline of the Soviet Union was also an important factor in their decision to act. Among the coup leaders were Gorbachev's Vice-President Genadii Yanaev and his Prime Minister Valentin Pavlov, Defence Minister Dimitrii Yazov, KGB Chief Vladimir Kryuchkov, and the Minister of the Interior, Boris Pugo.

Despite this impressive array of office-holders, the attempt to remove Gorbachev from power (he was on holiday in the Crimea at the time) failed because the army and the security forces refused to crush popular opposition to the plotters led by Boris Yeltsin (who had been elected President of Russia a couple of months before). But when Gorbachev returned to Moscow on 22 August 1991 he was soon faced with another 'coup', this time by Yeltsin. The Russian President seized control of key Soviet economic and financial institutions and began to manoeuvre to undermine the Gorbachev-devised Union treaty (which had been strongly endorsed by a popular referendum in March 1991). In December 1991 Yeltsin met with his presidential counterparts in the Ukraine and Belorussia and declared the establishment of a Commonwealth of Independent States (CIS). This was the kiss of death to the Union treaty and to the USSR.

In a televised broadcast on 25 December 1991 Gorbachev announced his resignation as Soviet President. He told his viewers:

We live in a new world. The cold war is finished. The arms race and the mad militarisation of states, which deformed our economy, society and values, has been stopped. The threat of world war has been lifted.

It was also a world in which the USSR no longer existed.

6 Conclusion
The Soviet factor in world politics, 1945–91

Three grand narrative themes have dominated the study of the Soviet role in postwar world politics.

First is the theme of bipolarity. This is the story of the division of Europe after the Second World War, of the cold war polarisation of world politics into two opposing armed camps, and the contest between the Soviet Union and the United States for power, prestige and position. It is a story, too, of the stabilisation of this bipolar split as each side came to recognise the need to limit competition and control conflict, above all to prevent the outbreak of general war involving the use of nuclear weapons. The USSR and the US dominated postwar international relations, although they were by no means the only significant actors in the international system. But bipolarism finally collapsed only with the decline and then self-destruction of the Soviet superpower.

Second is the theme of ideological competition. This is the story of communism versus capitalism, of the struggle between states, between economies, between political systems and between ideas and values. It is a story of Soviet expansionism and of the spread of communism after the Second World War. But it is a contest that was ultimately won by capitalism, which proved to be the more resilient, dynamic and durable system. The story ends with one side (communism) embracing the liberal ideology and democratic system of the other side (capitalism).

Third is the theme of system crisis. The focus in this story is on the internal weaknesses, contradictions and conflicts of the Soviet and communist system. In spite of the Soviet victory in the Second World War and the Soviet rise in world politics, the USSR was always a fragile superpower. Its internal regime survived only because it was authoritarian and repressive. The Soviet-dominated communist bloc was racked by constant crises and internal divisions. Nor could the USSR compete militarily with the United States without imposing an intolerable strain on a relatively weak and inefficient Soviet economy. In the end, it is argued, the cold war contest with the US served only to provide an external threat which could be used to legitimise the rule of a self-serving power elite and to provide this elite with an arena in which to fight out domestic political power struggles.

These narrative themes have an obvious relationship to the analytical perspectives on security, power, ideology and politics outlined at the beginning of this book. What one sees as the main driving force of Moscow's foreign policy largely determines how the big story is conceptualised. Furthermore, elements of each theme can be related and validated by reference to the detailed narrative of Soviet policy. It is also possible to identify aspects of the thinking of Soviet decision-makers which instantiate the impact on policy of concepts of bipolarism, ideological contest and system crisis.

However, it is important for historians to distinguish between these meta-narratives of Soviet foreign policy – the big, over-arching stories, as seen by outsider observers – from the way the actors themselves see the drama unfolding at the time. From the local and particular point of view the Soviet factor in world politics was a constantly changing variable, depending on the shifting perceptions and motivations of the relevant decision-makers. But it may be possible to discern a consistent series of outcomes – a long-term pattern or trend – arising from the continuity over time of the shared perceptions and motivations of Soviet leaders and decision-makers. The trend identified in this book has been the Soviet Union's constant striving to revolutionise the character of world politics. That revolutionary challenge bore no relation to the crude cold war caricature of a Soviet Union bent on world domination. While Moscow desired to remake the world in its own image the USSR pursued its ideological ambitions cautiously and was more a reactive than subversive power in global politics. The priority assigned to the building of socialism at home – which was defined by Moscow as the main Soviet contribution to the achievement of world socialism – was another brake on the pursuit of revolution. To that extent, the USSR was an upholder of the status quo as well as a revolutionary power. If elements of the extant international order suited Soviet interests then these were defended even at the cost of revolutionary interests. Such inclinations were reinforced by Soviet self-perceptions of their weakness and insecurity in the face of the external capitalist threat.

The Kremlin's combination of revolutionary ambition and conservative inclination engendered a contradictory and deeply ambiguous foreign policy and strategy. Indeed, that was another aspect of the Soviet factor in world politics: the uncertainty about Moscow's foreign policy goals. Was the aim of peaceful coexistence peace and coexistence or was it a means to a revolutionary end? Could east–west détente be maintained on a permanent basis when the Soviets aimed, in the long run, to subvert the international order? Gorbachev ended the uncertainty by abandoning the Soviet Union's revolutionary aspirations. But even he – a true product of the Soviet system – sought a revolutionary transformation of world politics, albeit one based on the practical implementation of liberal and humanistic values and goals.

The Soviet revolutionary challenge also engendered instability in world politics. But it was in many ways a predictable instability. Soviet ideological goals were not secret, nor was there any question of the Soviets forcibly imposing their ideological vision on the whole world. Moscow generally stuck to the treaties and agreements it made with the outside world. Even when it abrogated its international commitments the motives were usually reactive and defensive in character. The Soviet Union as an international actor rarely did anything surprising. Even such dramatic actions as blockading Berlin and the Cuban missile crisis were designed above all to provoke negotiation and compromise. Moscow always preferred political solutions to the problems and crises that it faced. Military action was always a last resort. The acuity of the Soviet sense of the cataclysmic danger of nuclear warfare was second to none.

Now that the USSR no longer exists, the uniqueness of the Soviet state as an actor in the international political system is becoming ever more clear. It was a state with leaders obsessed by national security who aspired to world revolution. It was a state which sought and achieved international influence and prestige but whose main goal remained the building of the socialist system at home. The biggest paradox of all was that the USSR was a state which challenged the global status quo but did so in a way that contributed to the order and predictability of world politics.

Biographical notes on major Soviet figures

Leonid I. Brezhnev (1906–82)

Joined the communist party in 1929. During the Second World War served as a political commissar on the Ukrainian front. Member of central committee from 1952 and the Presidium (Politburo) from 1957. Elected First Secretary of the CPSU in succession to Khrushchev in October 1964 (at the twenty-third party congress in March–April 1966 the title was changed to General Secretary and the Presidium reverted to its former title of Politburo). In June 1977 Brezhnev became Chairman of the Presidium of the Supreme Soviet (i.e. nominal head of state). When he died Brezhnev was succeeded by Yuri Andropov (November 1982) and then Konstantin Chernenko (February 1984).

Mikhail S. Gorbachev (1931–)

Became a candidate member of the CPSU in 1950 and a full member in 1952. Elected a member of the central committee at the twenty-fourth party congress in 1971. In 1978 appointed central committee member in charge of agriculture. In 1979 joined the Politburo as a candidate (i.e. non-voting) member and became full member in 1980. Elected General Secretary of the party in March 1985. Elected Chairman of the Supreme Soviet in May 1989, and President of the USSR by the Congress of People's Deputies in March 1990. Resigned as party leader following the attempted August Coup of 1991. Resigned as President of the USSR on 25 December 1991.

Andrei A. Gromyko (1909–89)

Joined the party in 1931. Member of the Soviet diplomatic corps from 1939. Served in the Soviet embassy in Washington during the war. In

1946–9 was the Soviet representative at the UN. Deputy Foreign Minister 1953–7. Soviet Foreign Minister 1957–85. Elected Chairman of the Presidium of the Supreme Soviet in 1985.

Nikita S. Khrushchev (1894–1971)

Active in the Ukraine during the revolutionary events of 1917. Joined the Bolshevik Party in 1918 and fought during the Russian civil war (1918–20). Elected to central committee in 1934. Head of the Moscow party organisation from 1935 and of the Ukrainian communist party from 1938. Member of the Politburo from 1939. During the war served as a political commissar on various fronts, including at Stalingrad. Returned to head the party in Moscow in 1949 and in 1950 took charge of agriculture. Elected First Secretary of the CPSU in September 1953. In February 1956 delivered his 'secret speech' denouncing Stalin at the twentieth party congress. In June 1957 defeated an attempt by hard-liners in the party leadership to replace him as First Secretary. Voted out of office by the Presidium and the central committee in October 1964. Spent his retirement composing his memoirs, which were first published in the west in the 1970s.

Vyacheslav M. Molotov (1890–1986)

An 'Old Bolshevik' (i.e. a pre-1917 member of the party) who served on the central committee and the Politburo from the early 1920s. From 1930 to 1941 was Chairman of the Council of People's Commissars (i.e. the Premier). Served as Soviet Foreign Minister 1939–49 and 1953–6. Removed from the party leadership following an unsuccessful attempt to oust Khrushchev from power. Expelled from the CPSU in 1962 following the twenty-second party congress at which Khrushchev publicly denounced him as a member of the 'anti-party group'.

Eduard A. Shevardnadze (1928–)

Joined the party in 1948. First Secretary of the Georgian communist party from 1972. Member of the central committee from 1976 and of the Politburo from 1978. In July 1985 succeeded Gromyko as Soviet Foreign Minister. Resigned from office in December 1990. Subsequently returned to Georgia to become President of the now-independent republic.

Joseph V. Stalin (1879–1953)

General Secretary of the Soviet communist party 1922–53.

Andrei A. Zhdanov (1896–1948)

Joined the Bolshevik Party in 1915. Member of the central committee from 1925 and of the Politburo from 1935. Headed the Leningrad party organisation 1934–45. In 1938 appointed chairman of the Foreign Affairs Commission of the Supreme Soviet. Chaired the Allied Control Commission in Finland 1944–5. In charge of the central committee's Departments of Agitation and Propaganda and Foreign Policy (later to become the International Department) 1945–8. Died of a heart attack.

Glossary of key terms

Cold war   The term used from 1947 onwards to describe the political and diplomatic conflict that had developed between the Soviet Union and the western powers after the Second World War.

Comecon   Western acronym for the **Council for Mutual Economic Assistance (CMEA)**.

Cominform   The Communist Information Bureau. Established in 1947 as a successor to the **Comintern**. Directed and coordinated the activities of the world's communist parties, especially in Europe. Abolished in 1956.

Comintern   The Communist International. Founded in Moscow in March 1919 as the world organisation of communist supporters of the Bolshevik Revolution in Russia. Abolished in 1943. Succeeded by **Cominform** in 1947.

Council for Mutual Economic Assistance (CMEA)   Soviet–east European trade and economic co-operation organisation founded in 1949. Later expanded to include Cuba and Vietnam. Soviet efforts to develop the CMEA into a supranational economic planning organisation were successfully opposed by other members. Disbanded in June 1991. Commonly called **Comecon** in the west.

Détente   A situation of lessened tension between two or more states signified by the amelioration of conflicts and differences and co-operative and friendly relations. The USSR sought détente throughout the cold war and there were many such periods of reduced tension, but it is conventional to designate the 1970s as the détente period in Soviet–American relations.

Grand Alliance   The coalition of Britain, the Soviet Union and the US which fought the Axis alliance of Germany, Italy and Japan during the Second World War.

Ideology   A set of related ideas. In the case of a political ideology the ideas will include a set of political goals and a programme for political action.

Marxism-Leninism   The official philosophical and political doctrine of the Soviet state. Derived from the ideas of Karl Marx, as interpreted and developed by Lenin and successive Soviet leaders and ideologues.

New Thinking   The rubric of Gorbachev's new approach to foreign policy and international relations in the mid-1980s.

Peaceful coexistence   The idea that the USSR could and should live peacefully side-by-side with capitalist states. The official policy of the Soviet state from 1920 onwards.

Politburo   The leading group of the Soviet communist party which ran the USSR. Between 1952 and 1966 the Politburo was called the **Presidium**.

Presidium   The name of the Soviet **Politburo** between 1952 and 1966.

Soviet ideology   Term that refers to the political ideology of the Soviet state which consisted of the core doctrine of **Marxism-Leninism**, together with the lessons and conclusions drawn from the practical, political application of that doctrine.

Two-camps doctrine   The view expounded by A.A. Zhdanov at the first conference of the **Cominform** in 1947 that the world had split into two camps – a democratic, peace-loving, socialist camp headed by the Soviet Union and a reactionary, aggressive, capitalist camp led by the United States. The doctrine was ditched in the 1950s when the Soviets saw the emergence of a zone of peace embracing a number of non-aligned third world countries as well as the progressive camp of socialist states.

Warsaw Pact   The military-political alliance of the Soviet–east European bloc. Established by a Treaty of Friendship, Co-operation and Mutual Assistance signed in Warsaw in May 1955. Disbanded in July 1991.

Guide to further reading

1 GENERAL HISTORIES

An excellent general history of Soviet foreign policy from 1917 to 1991 is Craig Nation (1992). Nogee & Donaldson (1988) offer a solid textbook on postwar Soviet foreign policy which contains a wealth of useful information and analyses. For an alternative perspective try Crockatt (1995) which combines historical interpretation with the application of international relations theory to the study of postwar Soviet (and American) foreign policy. Highly recommended, too, is Gaddis (1997) which situates Soviet foreign policy in its cold war context and reviews recent research and archival findings. For a general history of the cold war I would recommend Ashton (1989), Walker (1993) and LaFeber (1997). For an 'inside' view of postwar Soviet foreign policy see Ponomaryov et al. (1973) – an official, government-endorsed, textbook history. The official mindset of Soviet foreign policy is also exemplified by the works of Popov et al. (1975) and Sanakoyev and Kapchenko (1976). For outsider accounts of the Soviet ideology of foreign policy and international relations see Light (1988) and Jones (1990).

2 ORIGINS OF THE COLD WAR

There are three essential texts on Soviet foreign policy during the early years of the cold war: Kennedy-Pipe (1995), Mastny (1996) and Zubok and Pleshakov (1996). A very useful collection of detailed studies of the Soviet role in the outbreak of the cold war is Gori & Pons (1996). Some fascinating documentation is provided by Procacci (1994). Holloway (1994) integrates analysis of foreign policy with the fascinating story of the development of Soviet nuclear weapons. On the Korean War see Goncharov et al. (1993) and the articles by Katherine Weathersby.

3 THE KHRUSHCHEV ERA

The most studied event of the Khrushchev era is, of course, the Cuban missile crisis. A good place to start on the enormous literature on this topic is Garthoff (1989) and Fursenko and Naftali (1997). On the Sino-Soviet split, I have relied on the excellent documentary collections of Gittings (1968), Griffith (1964) and Hudson *et al.* (1961) and the recent documents and articles published in the bulletin of the Cold War International History Project (see p. 111). Khrushchev's memoirs (1971, 1974 and 1990) are fascinating, and by far the most revealing of any Soviet leader, particularly in relation to foreign policy.

4 DÉTENTE

My main guide through the era of détente has been Garthoff (1985), a monumental and immensely detailed account of Soviet (and American) foreign policy in the 1960s and 1970s. Edmonds (1975 and 1983), Steele (1985) and Ulam (1982) are also good general accounts of this period. The European dimension of détente is covered in detail in Sodaro (1991). On the character of Soviet foreign policy decision-taking under Brezhnev see the highly illuminating accounts of the invasion of Czechoslovakia in 1968 by Dawisha (1984), Valenta (1991) and Williams (articles 1994 and 1996). One of the most fascinating insider accounts of Soviet foreign policy under Brezhnev is Israelyan (1995). Israelyan, a historian as well as a professional diplomat, was a senior official in the Soviet foreign ministry at the time of the 1973 Middle East crisis. His account of the day-to-day workings of the Foreign Ministry and the activities of the Soviet leadership during this crisis really does tell how it actually was. On Soviet policy in the third world see Halliday (1982), Allison (1988), Golan (1988), Katz (1990), Patman (1990) and Light (1993).

5 GORBACHEV

Garthoff (1994) is another detailed and brilliant account, this time of Soviet and American foreign policies in the 1980s. A less comprehensive alternative to Garthoff is Oberdorfer (1992). Succinct summaries of Gorbachev's foreign policy may be found in Brown (1996) and White (1990), which also deal extensively with his domestic policies. Gorbachev's memoirs (Gorbachev, 1996) are much less revealing than you would expect. Far more rewarding are the speeches and articles in Gorbachev (1988) which convey a sense of the feeling as well as the ideas behind his New Thinking on Soviet foreign policy.

6 THE BIBLIOGRAPHY

The bibliography is mainly a compilation of the recent English-language literature on postwar Soviet foreign policy, written in the light of the considerable body of new evidence to emerge from the Russian archives since the late 1980s. In addition, I have included texts which I quote or make direct use of in this book. I have omitted a large number of older works on Soviet foreign policy, including some classic texts, but that is not meant to imply that they are without value or that they have not strongly influenced my views on the subject. In the memoirs sections I have included only the works of the main postwar Soviet leaders and foreign ministers.

7 THE COLD WAR INTERNATIONAL HISTORY PROJECT (CWIHP)

The articles section of the bibliography lists a rather large number of items published in the *Cold War International History Project Bulletin*. The CWIHP is based at the Woodrow Wilson International Center for Scholars in Washington, DC. It 'seeks to disseminate new information and perspectives on Cold War history emerging from previously inaccessible archives'. To this end the project publishes a bulletin which contains translations of newly accessed documents from the Russian and other archives together with extensive commentaries by some of the leading experts on the foreign policy of the USSR and the other socialist states. In this book I have relied very heavily on CWIHP documentation and analyses, in particular the work of Mark Kramer has been of inestimable value. CWIHP material can be accessed on the Internet at cwihp.si.edu.

Select bibliography

BOOKS

Allison, R., *The Soviet Union and the Strategy of Non-Alignment in the Third World*, Cambridge 1988.

Ashton, S.R., *In Search of Détente: The Politics of East–West Relations since 1945*, London 1989.

Bluth, C., *Soviet Strategic Arms Policy Before SALT*, Cambridge 1992.

Brown, A., *The Gorbachev Factor*, Oxford 1996.

Craig Nation, R., *Black Earth, Red Star: A History of Soviet Security Policy, 1917–1991*, Cornell 1992.

Crockatt, R., *The Fifty Years War: The United States and the Soviet Union in World Politics, 1941–1991*, London 1995.

Dawisha, K., *The Kremlin and the Prague Spring*, London 1984.

Edmonds, R., *Soviet Foreign Policy, 1962–1973*, Oxford 1975.

Edmonds, R., *Soviet Foreign Policy: The Brezhnev Years*, Oxford 1983.

Fursenko A. and Naftali, T., *'One Hell of a Gamble': Khrushchev, Castro, and Kennedy, 1958–1964*, New York 1997.

Gaddis, J.L., *The Long Peace: Inquiries into the History of the Cold War*, New York 1987.

Gaddis, J.L., *Russia, the Soviet Union and the United States*, 2nd edn, New York 1990.

Gaddis, J.L., *We Now Know: Rethinking Cold War History*, Oxford 1997.

Gaiduk, I.V., *The Soviet Union and the Vietnam War*, Chicago 1996.

Garthoff, R.L., *Détente and Confrontation: American–Soviet Relations from Nixon to Reagan*, Washington, DC 1985 (2nd edn, 1994).

Garthoff, R.L., *Reflections on the Cuban Missile Crisis*, rev. edn, Washington, DC 1989.

Garthoff, R.L., *The Great Transition: American–Soviet Relations and the End of the Cold War*, Washington, DC 1994.

George, A.L., *Managing U.S.–Soviet Rivalry: Problems of Crisis Prevention*, Westview Press 1983.

Gittings, J., *Survey of the Sino-Soviet Dispute*, London 1968.

Golan, G., *The Soviet Union and National Liberation Movements in the Third World*, London 1988.

Goncharov, S.N., Lewis, J.W. and Xue, Litai, *Uncertain Partners: Stalin, Mao and the Korean War*, Stanford 1993.

Gorbachev, M., *Perestroika: New Thinking for Our Country and the World*, London 1988.

Gori, F. and Pons, S. (eds), *The Soviet Union and Europe in the Cold War, 1943–53*, London 1996.

Griffith, W.E., *The Sino-Soviet Rift*, London 1964.

Halliday, F., *Threat from the East? Soviet Policy from Afghanistan and Iran to the Horn of Africa*, London 1982.

Halliday, F., *The Making of the Second Cold War*, 2nd edn, London 1986.

Haslam, J., *The Soviet Union and the Politics of Nuclear Weapons in Europe, 1969–1987*, London 1989

Holden, G., *The Warsaw Pact*, Oxford 1989.

Holloway, D., *The Soviet Union and the Arms Race*, 2nd edn, New Haven, Conn., 1988.

Holloway, D., *Stalin and the Bomb*, New Haven, Conn., 1994.

Hough, J.F., *The Struggle for the Third World*, Washington, DC 1986.

Hudson, G.F., Lowenthal, R. and MacFarquhar, R., *The Sino-Soviet Dispute*, New York 1961.

Israelyan, V., *Inside the Kremlin during the Yom Kippur War*, Pennsylvania 1995.

Jones, R.A., *The Soviet Concept of Limited Sovereignty from Lenin to Gorbachev: The Brezhnev Doctrine*, London 1990.

Katz, M.N. (ed.), *The USSR and Marxist Revolutions in the Third World*, Cambridge 1990.

Kennedy-Pipe, C., *Stalin's Cold War: Soviet Strategies in Europe, 1943–1956*, Manchester 1995.

LaFeber, W., *America, Russia and the Cold War, 1945–1996*, 8th edn, New York 1997.

Light, M., *The Soviet Theory of International Relations*, Brighton 1988.

Light, M., (ed.), *Troubled Friendships: Moscow's Third World Ventures*, London 1993.

Lynch, A., *The Soviet Study of International Relations*, Cambridge 1989.

McCagg, W.O., *Stalin Embattled, 1943–1948*, Detroit 1978.

Mastny, V., *The Cold War and Soviet Insecurity: The Stalin Years*, Oxford 1996.

Miller, N., *Soviet Relations with Latin America, 1959–1987*, Cambridge 1989.

Naimark, N., *The Russians in Germany: A History of the Soviet Zone of Occupation, 1945–1949*, Cambridge, Mass. 1995.

Naimark, N. and Gibianskii, L. (eds), *The Establishment of the Communist Regimes of Eastern Europe, 1944–1949*, Oxford 1997.

Nogee, J.L. and Donaldson, R.H., *Soviet Foreign Policy since World War II*, 3rd edn, New York 1988 (4th edn, 1992).

Oberdorfer, D., *The Turn: How the Cold War Came to an End*, London 1992.

Patman, R.G., *The Soviet Union in the Horn of Africa*, Cambridge 1990.

Ponomaryov, B., *et al. History of Soviet Foreign Policy, 1945–1970*, Moscow 1973.

Popov, V.I., *et al.* (eds), *A Study of Soviet Foreign Policy*, Moscow 1975.

Potichnyj, P.J. and Shapiro, J.P., (eds), *From Cold War to Détente*, New York 1976.

Procacci G., (ed.), *The Cominform: Minutes of the Three Conferences,* Milan 1994

Rhodes, James, R., (ed.), *The Czechoslovak Crisis 1968*, London 1969.

Richardson, J.L., *Germany and the Atlantic Alliance*, Cambridge, Mass. 1966.

Sanakoyev, Sh.P. and Kapchenko, N.I., *Socialism: Foreign Policy in Theory and Practice*, Moscow 1976.

Savelyev, A.G. and Detinov, N.N., *The Big Five: Arms Control Decision-Making in the Soviet Union*, Westport 1995.

Shenfield, S., *The Nuclear Predicament: Explorations in Soviet Ideology*, London 1987.

Sherr, A.B., *The Other Side of Arms Control: Soviet Objectives in the Gorbachev Era*, London 1988.

Shulman, M.D., *Stalin's Foreign Policy Reappraised*, Cambridge, Mass. 1963.

Sodaro, M.J., *Moscow, Germany, and the West from Khrushchev to Gorbachev*, London 1991.

Steele, J., *The Limits of Soviet Power*, London 1985.

Swain, G. and Swain, N., *Eastern Europe since 1945*, London 1995.

Thompson, W., *The World Communist Movement since 1945*, London 1997.

Ulam, A.B., *Expansion and Coexistence: Soviet Foreign Policy, 1917–1973*, New York 1971.

Ulam, A.B., *Dangerous Relations: The Soviet Union in World Politics, 1970–82*, New York 1982.

Valenta, J., *Soviet Intervention in Czechoslovakia, 1968: Anatomy of a Decision*, rev. edn, Baltimore 1991.

Valenta, J. and Potter, W. (eds), *Soviet Decisionmaking for National Security*, London 1984.

Van Ree, E., *Socialism in One Zone: Stalin's Policy in Korea, 1945–1947*, Oxford 1989.

Walker, M., *The Cold War*, London 1993.

Werth, A., *Russia: The Post-War Years*, London 1971.

Westad, O.A., (ed.), *The Fall of Détente: Soviet–American Relations in the Carter Years*, Scandinavian University Press 1997.

Westad, O.A., Holtsmark, S. and Neumann, I.B. (eds), *The Soviet Union in Eastern Europe, 1945–1989*, London 1994.

White, S., *Gorbachev in Power*, Cambridge 1990.

Zagoria, D.S., *The Sino-Soviet Conflict, 1956–1961*, Princeton, NJ 1962.

Zimmerman, W., *Soviet Perspectives on International Relations, 1956–1967*, Princeton, NJ 1969.

Zubok, V. and Pleshakov, C., *Inside the Kremlin's Cold War*, Cambridge, Mass. 1996.

ARTICLES

Blacker, C.D., 'The Kremlin and Détente: Soviet Conceptions, Hopes and Expectations' in A.L. George (ed.), *Managing U.S.–Soviet Rivalry*, Westview Press 1983.
Brus, W., 'Stalinism and the "People's Democracies"' in R.C. Tucker (ed.), *Stalinism: Essays in Historical Interpretation*, New York 1977.
Cimbala, S.J., 'Command, Control and Cuban Missiles: A Crisis Revisited', *Journal of Slavic Military Studies*, vol. 10, no. 1, 1997.
Dallin, A., 'The Soviet Union as a Revolutionary Power' in C. Merridale and C. Ward (eds), *Perestroika: The Historical Perspective*, London 1991.
Fursenko, A. and Naftali, T. 'The Pitsunda Decision: Khrushchev and Nuclear Weapons', *Cold War International History Project Bulletin*, no. 10, March 1998.
Gaiduk, I.V., 'The Vietnam War and Soviet–American Relations, 1964–73: New Russian Evidence', *Cold War International History Project Bulletin*, nos. 6–7, Winter 1995–6.
Gaiduk, I.V., 'Soviet Policy towards US Participation in the Vietnam War', *History*, vol. 81, no. 261, 1996.
Garthoff, R.L., 'Cuban Missile Crisis: The Soviet Story', *Foreign Policy*, Fall 1988.
Gibianskii, L., 'The Soviet Bloc and the Initial Stage of the Cold War: Archival Documents on Stalin's Meetings with Communist Leaders of Yugoslavia and Bulgaria, 1946–1948', *Cold War International History Project Bulletin*, no. 10, March 1998.
Gluchowski, L.W., 'Poland, 1956: Khrushchev, Gomulka, and the "Polish October"', *Cold War International History Project Bulletin*, no. 5, Spring 1995.
Granville, S., 'Tito and the Nagy Affair in 1956', *East European Quarterly*, March 1998.
Harrison, H.M., 'Soviet–East German Relations after World War II', *Problems of Post-Communism*, vol. 42, no. 5, 1995.
Kaplan, K. and Mastny, V., 'Stalin, Czechoslovakia, and the Marshall Plan: New Documentation from Czechoslovak Archives', *Bohemia Band 32*, 1991.
Korobochkin, M., 'Soviet Policy Toward Finland and Norway, 1947–1949', *Scandinavian Journal of History*, vol. 20, no. 3, 1995.
Kramer, M., 'New Sources on the 1968 Soviet Invasion of Czechoslovakia', *Cold War International History Project Bulletin*, nos. 2 and 3, 1992–3.
Kramer, M., 'Tactical Nuclear Weapons, Soviet Command Authority and the Cuban Missile Crisis', *International History Review*, November 1993.

Kramer, M., 'Poland, 1980–81: Soviet Policy During the Polish Crisis', *Cold War International History Project Bulletin*, no. 5, Spring 1995.

Kramer, M., 'The Soviet Foreign Ministry Appraisal of Sino-Soviet Relations on the Eve of the Split', *Cold War International History Project Bulletin*, nos. 6–7, Winter 1995–6.

Kramer, M., 'New Evidence on Soviet Decision-Making and the 1956 Polish and Hungarian Crises', *Cold War International History Project Bulletin*, nos. 8–9, Winter 1996–7.

Kramer, M., 'The Soviet Union and Eastern Europe: Spheres of Influence' in N. Woods (ed.), *Explaining International Relations since 1945*, Oxford 1997.

Kramer, M., 'Declassified Materials from CPSU Central Committee Plenums: Sources, Contexts, Highlights', *Cold War International History Project Bulletin*, no. 10, March 1998a.

Kramer, M., 'The Soviet Union and the 1956 Crises in Hungary and Poland: Reassessments and New Findings', *Journal of Contemporary History*, vol. 33, no. 2, 1998b.

Leffler, M.P., 'Inside Enemy Archives: The Cold War Reopened', *Foreign Affairs*, vol. 75, no. 4, July–August 1996.

Light, M., 'Restructuring Soviet Foreign Policy' in R.J. Hill and J.A. Dellenbrant (eds), *Gorbachev and Perestroika*, London 1989.

Mansourov, A.Y., 'Stalin, Mao, Kim and China's Decision to Enter the Korean War: New Evidence from Russian Archives', *Cold War International History Project Bulletin*, nos. 6–7, Winter 1995–6.

Musatov, V., 'The Inside Story of the Invasion', *New Times*, no. 16, 1992.

Nevakivi, J., 'A Decisive Armistice 1944–1947: Why Was Finland Not Sovietized?', *Scandinavian Journal of History*, vol. 19, no. 2, 1994.

Ostermann, C.F., 'New Evidence on the Sino-Soviet Border Dispute, 1969–1971', *Cold War International History Project Bulletin*, nos. 6–7, Winter 1995–6.

Ostermann, C.F., '"This Is Not A Politburo, But A Madhouse": The Post-Stalin Succession Struggle, Soviet Deutschlandpolitik and the SED: New Evidence from Russian, German and Hungarian Archives', *Cold War International History Project Bulletin*, no. 10, March 1998.

Parrish, S., 'Soviet Reaction to the Marshall Plan: Opportunity or Threat?', *Problems of Post-Communism*, vol. 42, no. 5, 1995.

Pravda, A., 'The Politics of Foreign Policy' in S. White, A. Pravda and Z. Gitelman (eds), *Developments in Soviet and Post-Soviet Politics*, 2nd edn, London 1992.

Rainer, J.M., 'The Road to Budapest 1956: New Documentation on the Kremlin's Decision to Intervene', *Hungarian Quarterly*, vol. 37, nos. 142–3, 1996.

Richter, J., 'Re-examining Soviet Policy Towards Germany in 1953', *Europe-Asia Studies*, vol. 45, no. 4, 1993.

Roberts, G., 'Moscow and the Marshall Plan: Politics, Ideology and the Onset of Cold War, 1947', *Europe-Asia Studies*, December 1994.

Roberts, G., 'Stalin and the Cold War', *Europe-Asia Studies*, December 1997.

Sassoon, D., 'The Rise and Fall of West European Communism', *Contemporary European History*, vol. 1, no. 2, 1992.

Staritz, D., 'The SED, Stalin and the German Question: Interests and Decision-Making in the Light of New Sources', *German History*, vol. 10, no. 3, 1992.

Steele, J., 'The Soviet Union: What Happened to Détente?' in N. Chomsky, J. Steele and J. Gittings, *Superpowers in Collision: The Cold War Now*, London 1982.

Swain, G., 'Stalin's Wartime Vision of the Postwar World', *Diplomacy and Statecraft*, vol. 7, no. 1, 1996.

Tischler, J., 'Interconnections: Poland's October and the 1956 Hungarian Revolution', *Hungarian Quarterly*, vol. 38, Spring 1997.

Weathersby, K., 'New Findings on the Korean War', *Cold War International History Project Bulletin*, no. 3, Fall 1993.

Weathersby, K., 'New Russian Archival Materials, Old American Debates, and the Korean War', *Problems of Post-Communism*, vol. 42, no. 5, 1995.

Weathersby, K., 'New Russian Documents on the Korean War', *Cold War International History Project Bulletin*, nos. 6–7, Winter 1995–6.

Westad, O.A., 'Prelude to Invasion: The Soviet Union and Afghan Communists, 1978–1979', *International History Review*, February 1994.

Westad, O.A., 'Moscow and the Angolan Crisis: A New Pattern of Intervention', *Cold War International History Project Bulletin*, nos. 8–9, Winter 1996–7a.

Westad, O.A., 'New Russian Evidence on the Soviet Intervention in Afghanistan', *Cold War International History Project Bulletin*, nos. 8–9, Winter 1996–7b.

Wettig, G., 'Stalin and German Reunification: Archival Evidence on Soviet Foreign Policy in Spring 1952', *Historical Journal*, vol. 37, no. 2, 1994.

Williams, K., 'Political Love's Labours Lost: Negotiations between Prague and Moscow in 1968', *Slovo*, March 1994.

Williams, K., 'New Sources on Soviet Decision Making during the 1968 Czechoslovak Crisis', *Europe-Asia Studies*, vol. 48, no. 3, 1996.

Wohlforth, W.C., 'New Evidence on Moscow's Cold War: Ambiguity in Search of Theory', *Diplomatic History*, vol. 21, no. 2, 1997.

Zubok, V.M., 'Soviet Activities in Europe after World War II', *Problems of Post-Communism*, vol. 42, no. 5, 1995.

Zubok, V.M., 'CPSU Plenums, Leadership Struggles and Soviet Cold War Politics', *Cold War International History Project Bulletin*, no. 10, March 1998.

MEMOIRS

Gorbachev, M., *Mikhail Gorbachev: Memoirs*, London 1996.
Gromyko, A., *Memories*, London 1989.
Khrushchev, N., *Khrushchev Remembers*, London 1971.
Khrushchev, N., *Khrushchev Remembers: The Last Testament*, London 1974.
Khrushchev, N., *Khrushchev Remembers: The Glasnost Tapes*, Boston 1990.
Molotov Remembers: Inside Kremlin Politics: Conversations with Felix Chuev (intro. A. Resis), Chicago 1993.
Shevardnadze, E., *The Future Belongs to Freedom*, London 1991.

UNPUBLISHED SOURCES

Buckley, C., 'The Caribbean Crisis, 1962: The Soviet Perspective', MA thesis, University College Cork 1995.
Lyons, D.J., 'Soviet Decisions for Military Intervention: Case Studies in Soviet Foreign Policy Decision Making', MPhil thesis, University College Cork 1996.
McGee, B.J., 'Anglo-Soviet Relations, 1945–1947', MA thesis, University College Cork 1997.
Quinn, B., 'The Cominform and its Position in Soviet Foreign Policy', MA thesis, University College Cork 1997.

Index

Lightning Source UK Ltd.
Milton Keynes UK
UKOW040500131012

200486UK00001B/10/A